Tensions in the Church
Facing the Challenges, Seizing the Opportunities

James J. Bacik

Sheed & Ward

Sheed & Ward™ is a service of The National Catholic Reporter Publishing Company.

Library of Congress Cataloguing in Publication Data

Bacik, James J., 1936-
    Tensions in the Church : facing the challenges, seizing the opportunities / James J. Bacik
        p.   cm.
    ISBN 1-55612-624-7 (alk. paper)
    1. Catholic Church--North America--History--1965- 2. Catholic Church--North America--Doctrines--History--20th century.
    3. Religious pluralism--Catholic Church--History--20th century.
    4. Catholic Church--Liturgy--History--20th century. 5. Pastoral theology--Catholic Church. 6. Catholic Church--Relations.
    I. Title
    BX1403.2.B33   1993
    230'.2--dc20   92-46309
                                                              CIP

Published by: Sheed & Ward
                115 E. Armour Blvd.
                P.O. Box 419492
                Kansas City, MO 64141-6492

To order, call: (800) 333-7373

For my sister, Barbara Bacik Wallace,
faithful conserver of the family traditions,
master teacher who inspires theologians
to attend to their own well-being,
spontaneous witness
to the graciousness of the Mystery.

Contents

Foreword

Because James Bacik has served for most of his priestly life as a campus minister rather than in a tenured university professorship, his theological credentials, gifts, and accomplishments may still be too little known and appreciated within the U.S. Catholic community. If this is the case, I hope this book will help to bring his name and his work to the attention of a much wider audience, because the truth is that James Bacik is one of North America's finest, most insightful theologians, with a remarkable capacity for clear writing and effective teaching.

Tensions in the Church reminds us once again that theology is not simply an academic discipline. According to St. Anselm's classic definition, theology is "faith seeking understanding" and as such must always be ecclesial and pastoral in intention, in tone, and in outlook. The essays in this book are designed to connect inquiring and alienated Catholics with the fruits of the best of contemporary theological scholarship. Some of the most compelling material is presented in the form of letters to individuals who are returning to the Church, thinking of leaving it, or already on the outside looking back in.

In the process he touches almost all the major issues that are at the root of today's "tensions" in the Church: ordination of women, the Vatican's directives on sexual and medical ethics, theological dissent, the challenge of pluralism, papal authority, changes in the liturgy, the crisis of the priesthood, the encroachments of fundamentalism, and so forth. And he treats these issues in a consistently balanced and even-handed manner.

But James Bacik is neither a generic theologian nor a generic Christian. He is a committed "Catholic without embarrassment," to use the title of one of his essays. "There is," he writes, "a way to be proudly Catholic without being arrogant, to be open-minded without being mindless, . . . to be true to one's heritage without being exclusive." It is a Catholicism that is at once committed and critical, loyal and yet open to dissent.

"We human beings are obliged to be responsible dissenters," he points out, "since we are called by God not simply to conform to institutional standards, but to respond freely to the divine summons which echoes in our hearts. As responsible social creatures, we must be concerned about those who suffer from institutional discrimination. Our dedication to Christ is lived out in a Church which has made mistakes in the past and which is committed to continuous reform in the light of the gospel."

Father Bacik, however, recognizes the "fundamental ambivalence" in all forms of institutional religion, and not just in Catholicism. "[Religion] can be a force for good or for evil; it can legitimate unjust situations or call for reform; it can promote superstition or liberate people for intelligent inquiry; it can foster prejudice or teach equality; it can help keep people in an infantile state or enable them to move toward maturity; it can enslave or liberate; it can encourage a narrow exclusivism or foster a healthy open-mindedness; it can cause neurotic guilt feelings or produce a healthy sense of creaturehood; it can cause suffering or work to reduce it. In short, religion can diminish or promote the truly human."

This mature and healthy theological perspective has informed all of James Bacik's work: as campus minister at Bowling Green and the University of Toledo, as a teacher, preacher, and pastor, and as a writer of scholarly and popular books and articles. In an essay written on the occasion of his 25th anniversary of ordination to the priesthood, he acknowledged "an abiding sense that the ministry is intrinsically worthwhile," that it offers "a hardened and fragmented world" the Christian message of "reconciliation and hope," and that it can help to make it "possible for human beings to live in peace and harmony, working for the common good in a cooperative way."

This book is not only an exercise in theological reflection; it is an exercise in ministry. James Bacik excels at both.

—Richard P. McBrien

Introduction

FROM THE VERY BEGINNING, THE CHURCH, WHICH IS CALLED TO BE A
sign of unity and harmony, has been plagued with disruptive
tensions. Life in the church has never been without controversies,
strains, frustrations, stresses, quarrels, disagreements and even
hostilities. In this regard, Paul's Letters to the Corinthians are
more revealing than Luke's idyllic picture of the early church in
Acts. Dialectical descriptions of the church as graced but sinful
capture more of the experience of its members than does the
image of the church as a perfect society or as the spotless bride
of Christ.

Today, we are more aware of the tensions in the church.
Serious strains and hostilities attract the attention of the media.
Individuals who have developed a sense of co-responsibility for
the church are now more attuned to the frustrations occasioned
by its failed ideals. The formation of distinct interest groups has
brought to light the hidden stresses which always exist in pluralistic communities. Members tutored by Vatican II are more
likely to express their deep feelings and honest opinions about
disputed church matters.

Pope John XXIII called the Council to initiate a spiritual renewal which would enable the church to radiate the splendor of
God and the love of Christ to the world. But tensions within the

body of bishops gathered at the Council soon became evident. In some cases, the differences were reconciled in a workable synthesis which preserved the interests of competing groups. The final draft of the Dogmatic Constitution on Divine Revelation, for example, presented God as the ultimate source of revelation, a comprehensive theological perspective which compelled assent from both liberal and conservative bishops. In other cases, however, the bishops and their expert advisors were not able to achieve a theological synthesis. In these cases they often resorted to compromises in which the fundamental perspectives and insights of each side were included in the final documents. Thus, the Dogmatic Constitution on the Church includes a chapter on the church as the People of God and one on the hierarchical structure of the church, but fails to synthesize these two emphases in a mutually acceptable, comprehensive theological perspective. This strategy of compromise, necessary at the time to secure substantial majorities for the documents, has left us with fundamental tensions today. On many disputed questions, each side can quote the documents to support its position.

We also have fundamental differences over the interpretation of the post-conciliar period. Some Catholics are convinced that the renewal has gone badly because liberal groups have distorted the teachings and intent of the Council. Others claim that the general direction of church reform is on target, and that we must continue to be faithful to the spirit of Vatican II, despite reactionary objections. Many of the tensions we experience today are fueled by these two diverse outlooks on developments in the church since the end of the Council.

In one of its great achievements, "The Pastoral Constitution on the Church in the Modern World," Vatican II called for active engagement of Catholics in the contemporary world. Most Catholics agree on the general principle that the church should be an instrument of the kingdom in the world. Serious disagreements arise, however, about the appropriate approaches and methods for carrying out this task. Avery Dulles has put some conceptual order into the discussion by distinguishing traditionalists, neoconservatives, liberals and radicals (cf. "Catholicism and American Culture: The Uneasy Dialogue," in *America*, Jan. 27, 1990). Traditionalists are highly critical of the dominant culture and want to restore a more authoritarian Catholicism to combat societal evils. Neo-conservatives insist that the church should draw on its liturgical, theological and moral heritage in order to promote the American experiment in ordered liberty and enhance our system of democratic capitalism. Liberals are convinced that our American tradition of participatory democracy and fundamental freedom should become more completely incorporated into the life of the church, making it a more credible witness to Gospel values and a more effective instrument for transforming society. Finally, Dulles identifies the radicals, who adopt a vigorous counter-cultural stance by speaking out against capitalism, consumerism, militarism, racism and the rape of the environment. Tensions among these diverse groups escalate when the discussion turns to difficult public policy questions, such as abortion, or economic development.

Since the close of Vatican II, it has become more evident that we are living through a transition period in which the modern world is breaking up and a new world, often vaguely termed "post-modern," is being formed. Modernity, which celebrated the autonomy of reason and the effectiveness of the scientific method, has failed to give us the kind of human progress that we desperately need and truly desire. It has perpetuated patriarchy, supported colonialism, harmed the environment and fostered individualism. The secularism associated with modernity, which reduces the truth to what can be empirically verified, has failed to satisfy the deeper longings of the human spirit.

The growing awareness of the collapse of the modern world has created new tensions in the church. Some see it as an opportunity to return to a pre-modern Catholicism characterized by strong centralized control from the Vatican and by a firm stand against the destructive developments of modernity. Others view the situation as an opportunity to develop a new style of Catholicism, which unites all members of the church in a common effort to care for the environment, to promote healthy relationships and to make the church a genuine dialogue partner in creating a better society. This tension is ultimately based in competing ecclesiologies. Both use the language of communion and community, but one side emphasizes the necessary hierarchical structure of communal church life, while the other puts the stress on mutuality, co-responsibility and fundamental equality within the faith community.

Catholics experience some tensions simply by participating in the life of the local church. At a very fundamental level, we worship, learn and serve together as males and females, influenced by the gender differences prevalent in our society. The ordinary strains built into male-female relations in our culture are intensified in a church which excludes women from full participation. The development of distinctive feminine and masculine spiritualities has, in the short term, increased the frustrations of many women and some men in the church, even though these gender-based spiritualities hold open the possibilities for more satisfying modes of collaboration in the future.

Historically, there have always been tensions between ordained leaders of parishes and the other baptized members. In the United States, this relationship has been colored by the prominent role of the laity in founding and organizing parishes in the early years of our national history and by the subsequent vigorous clerical reaction to lay control of parish finances. The Second Vatican Council ushered in new developments in this complex relationship. Lay ministry has flourished as never before in history. Leaders have emerged who are not officially ordained, but who exercise great influence on parish life. New forms of collaborative ministry have been developed. Fewer pastors are functioning as autonomous authority figures, and more are sharing power by relying on the cooperation of other committed leaders. In many cases these developments have enriched parish life and facilitated the personal growth of pastoral ministers. On the other hand, new tensions have arisen. Collaboration is difficult when leaders within a parish have different mindsets and espouse theologies which are hard to reconcile. Lay ministers who interact with authoritarian pastors are often frustrated, as are pastors who work with poorly trained leaders. Busy parish leaders know the strain of balancing their active life of service and their need for a nourishing contemplative life. Many leaders who must work through long hours of group process are frustrated that they cannot spend more time ministering directly to individuals. Lay persons, who take seriously their baptismal responsibilities for the well-being of the church, often have difficulty balancing the time they spend at work, with family and in parish activities. This tension has been intensified by the Council's call for greater lay involvement in the life of the church and by zealous pastors who either knowingly or inadvertently pressure their parishioners to get more involved. Recognizing this problem, concerned church members have called for greater emphasis on service to the world to balance all the attention that has been given to internal church ministries. Within parishes it is possible to discern various subgroupings which all too often have trouble getting along with one another. At the extremes are a small number of reactionary Catholics, who actively oppose the reforms of the Council, and a few radicals, who maintain a loose relationship with the church, but in reality have rejected its fundamental teachings. Within the mainstream, we have a continuing tension between conservatives, who insist on a hierarchical model of the church which preserves the tradition, and liberals, who favor a communal model which celebrates co-responsibility and adaptation. Charismatic Catholics often find themselves at odds with both conservatives and liberal members of the church, who are uncomfortable with their "born again" language and more emotional piety. Individuals who are very involved in transparochial movements, such as Cursillo, at times have trouble relating to their parishes and finding time to be involved in them. The presence of Opus Dei members in a parish can produce anxiety among parishioners who question their secrecy and conservative agenda. In some parishes, diverse groups have learned to work together; but in many others, they remain divided, undermining the unity which should characterize parish life.

Much of the tension in the church today occurs when individuals feel trapped in the middle of competing forces. For example, bishops are often caught between the conservative Vatican bureaucracy influenced by a few American reactionaries, and the majority of the people in their dioceses, who are more moderate in their views. Pastors face the challenge of presenting official church teaching on topics such as birth control and *in vitro* fertilization to their parishioners who have already rejected the Vatican positions. Pastoral leaders know the frustration of trying to enforce diocesan guidelines on pastoral practices, such as Confession before First Communion, against the desires of parents who disagree with the official policy. Laypersons can feel caught in the middle when trying to explain the church's official positions on issues such as premarital sex and abortion to friends and offspring who disagree with the stance of the hierarchy.

The word "tension" captures a lot of the experience of living in the church today. All segments of the church—from laypersons to the hierarchy—feel the stress. As individuals, we know the discomfort of trying to respond to competing voices. Groups experience estrangement as well as the temptation to alienate others. Even in facing the destructive tendencies in our culture, we cannot achieve a united front, but remain divided on the best strategies.

In an age of cultural transition and church renewal, certain tensions are inevitably intensified. Our common challenge is to keep these tensions from devolving into hostile attitudes and destructive attacks. The Catholic church should not be a battle ground in which fellow believers are perceived as the enemy. On the contrary, we must strive to live up to the ideal of unity in diversity, which has always been part of our Catholic heritage. The Catholic community should be the home of an impassioned quest for truth and wisdom, which does not impugn the motives of those who disagree. We need to search together for a redefinition of Catholic identity that is at once faithful to our heritage and intelligible to the post-modern world. We need collaborative approaches to develop more effective pastoral strategies, which learn from the past and respond creatively to the current challenges. Tensions need not be destructive and deadening; they can be fruitful and energizing.

The essays in this book represent my own efforts to respond to the tensions that are part of my experience as the co-pastor of a university parish and as a theologian often called to present a popularized version of what the great thinkers have said. The essays were originally circulated privately as a catalyst for personal reflection and group discussion. My hope is that collected here they will serve this same function for a wider audience.

The theological perspective evidenced throughout this book is shaped by the work of the great German Jesuit, Karl Rahner, one of the most influential theologians in the history of the church. Early in my ministry as a priest, I discovered, almost by accident, that Rahner's thought contains valuable insights which are extremely useful in preaching, teaching and counseling. Later, I made a more careful study of his theology in my book, *Apologetics and the Eclipse of Mystery*, (University of Notre Dame Press, 1978), which solidified my intuitive sense that Rahner's framework and methodology are particularly well-suited for meeting contemporary pastoral needs, including the challenge of dealing with tensions in the church.

Rahner teaches us to ask questions, to probe cultural trends, to examine personal experiences, and to search the broad Christian tradition for wisdom. There is an autobiographical strain in Rahner's writings which reveals him as an honest searcher, not content with pat answers. His sober realism and wintry piety encourages us to face life on its own terms, and to avoid utopian thinking. He encourages us to accept the inevitability of tensions in life, but at the same time he calls us to recognize our capacity to make them more fruitful. His sophisticated method of correlation reminds us that the proclamation of the Christian message must be a response to the genuine concerns of people today. It is not enough to present a beautiful doctrine of the church which ignores the tensions experienced by its members. Finally, Rahner has carefully balanced and related the notion of a universal revelation available to all people with the conviction that the revelatory process reached a definitive high point in Jesus of Nazareth. The church has the essential task of proclaiming Christ as the Final Prophet who can illumine the experience of every human being. From this perspective, we cannot escape the tensions of church life either by an uncritical fundamentalism, which turns every church statement into an infallible dogma, or by a mindless relativism, which suggests that every insight and opinion has equal validity. On the contrary, we must work our way through the tensions, searching for a fruitful synthesis, which holds on to what is true and good in the competing forces. Concretely, we must take seriously both the authoritative tradition and the personal experiences of people today without denying either one.

In my own pastoral work, I find that I often make use of the insights of other theologians and scholars. My book, *Contemporary Theologians* (Thomas More Press, 1988; Triumph Press, 1991), examines the ways that influential theologians such as Hans Küng, Bernard Lonergan and John Courtney Murray help us to deal with important existential concerns. In responding to the challenge of tensions in the church, I have used popularized versions of the thinking of these theologians as well as scholars from other disciplines. My usual procedure is to incorporate their insights into the larger perspective provided by Rahner.

The articles in this book are clustered around four particular areas of tension in the church today: dissent, polarization, ministry and ecumenical relationships.

Chapter One examines the tensions created by public dissent in the church. Dissent is widespread and comes from both the left and the right. For many people, the Charles Curran case focused the issues in a concrete and graphic way. Commentators still debate the significance of this case for the church as a whole.

Rendering the tensions over dissent fruitful requires a comprehensive perspective which respects both the authority of the magisterium and the rights of personal conscience. Karl Rahner's famous article on the "World Church" places the question of dissent in the context of an evolving church, which is moving towards greater decentralization and more autonomy for local churches. In this situation, theologians bear a heavy responsibility to debate controversial issues and to criticize opinions that are not faithful to the tradition.

Within this general framework, the essays in this chapter propose a number of propositions. Dissent can and has enriched the life of the church. It is important to distinguish dogmas, which command assent of all Catholics, and doctrines, which call for acceptance, but, in principle, admit of dissent. Dissent must always be carried out responsibly after prayerful reflection and with concern for the sensibilities of other members of the church.

The first chapter also treats common grievances voiced by ordinary Catholics. Cases where persons have been hurt and alienated are, indeed, sad and regrettable. We must reach out to these people with compassion. In some situations, individuals are still reacting against a pre-Vatican II church, which has already made important strides in reforming itself. We must inform these persons about the progress made in the post-conciliar church and invite them to participate in the continuing reform.

Resolving these tensions requires understanding and charity on the part of all. The more faithful we are as a church to the good news proclaimed by Jesus Christ, the more credible and attractive we become. The better job we do of reformulating and proclaiming the essential Christian truths, the better chance we have of attracting back to the church the serious searchers who have rejected questionable formulations of traditional teaching.

Chapter Two explores the unavoidable tensions which surface as Catholics search for a unified identity in a pluralistic church. Unfortunately, we are experiencing a growing polarization which focuses on the differences and turns those who disagree into enemies.

Greater conceptual clarity will help us manage these tensions in a more constructive way. Some Catholics work out of a classical mindset or worldview, which sees reality as static and truth as timeless. Other Catholics have developed a contemporary mindset, which emphasizes that the world is evolving and that truth is historically, culturally and personally conditioned. These distinct mindsets, in turn, form the basis for a person's philosophy, theology, spirituality and lifestyle. Many of our disagreements on specific questions flow out of these fundamentally different approaches to life.

Our growing awareness of pluralism and diversity has prompted a new effort to define Catholic identity in a contemporary context. Many authors give great prominence to the Catholic incarnational or sacramental sense, which is attuned to the presence of the infinite in the finite both in the everyday world and our liturgical gatherings. The Catholic imagination also has a strong sense of tradition, an appreciation of the unifying role of the Papacy and a fundamentally positive outlook on human nature. By focusing on these and other general characteristics or sensibilities, rather than on disputed doctrinal interpretations, we are in a better position to find common elements which can ground a viable Catholic identity.

Unity-in-diversity is a high ideal which still has power to attract Catholics today. It suggests that we unite around essentials, give freedom in accidental matters and try to maintain charity in all our interactions. This traditional wisdom provides an over-arching strategy for transforming polarized groups into unified communities.

Chapter Three takes up some of the tensions connected with the post-conciliar efforts to improve church ministry and enhance liturgical celebrations. Strains persist between clergy and laity as they work out their respective roles in the church. Some priests are still uncomfortable with the collaborative style of ministry developed since the Council. Many pastoral ministers are feeling drained by the escalating demands of contemporary parish life.

These tensions can become more fruitful when pastoral leaders are able to collaborate on the basis of mutual respect and are open to receiving from others as well as giving. This style of ministry can be energizing and illuminating. Contemporary theology encourages us to move in this direction. The church is a community in which all members are co-responsible for its well-being. Through baptism, all the members share in the priesthood of Christ and are called to a life of holiness. Ministers are chosen not for advantage but for service. Through ordination, a member of the church is designated and empowered as the official servant-leader of the faith community. A parish which embodies these theological themes creates a climate in which ministers not only serve others, but can also find nourishment for themselves.

Liturgical reforms have been widely accepted within the church. Nevertheless, some tensions still remain. Leaving aside reactionaries who oppose all changes, we still find a sizable number of Catholics who feel that the contemporary liturgy lacks a proper sense of mystery and reverence. Others are comfortable with the general direction of the reform, but want to see even more flexibility and adaptation. Liturgical planners in parishes are under a good deal of pressure to satisfy the desires of these two groups. Furthermore, pastoral ministers, who are trying to respond to the practical needs of their people, sometimes find themselves at odds with the liturgical purists, who are guided more by the inner logic of the rites themselves. Questions about pastoral adaptations of some of the rituals connected with the revised RCIA program give focus to these tensions.

A solid theology of the sacraments is needed to resolve these tensions. Following the lead of Karl Rahner, we can say that sacraments are the visibility of divine grace, which is always and everywhere operative within the human family. They are special encounters with the Risen Lord, which remind us of all the ways that God is healing and nourishing people. Through the sacraments, the church actualizes itself, becoming, in the process, a visible sign of the presence of the kingdom in the world. In this approach to the sacraments, two points must be maintained: the universality of grace and the importance of sacramental rites. As bodily, imaginative, social creatures, we need perceptible reminders of God's presence and opportunities to gather with others to celebrate it. The sacramental life of the church shapes our consciousness and gives direction to our service to the world.

Within this theological framework, the essays in the second half of this chapter examine the importance and purpose of liturgical participation and suggest ways to enhance our sense of the Gracious Mystery in our liturgies.

Chapter Four deals with tensions in the church created by ecumenical and interfaith encounters. Today, church members often find themselves confronted by fundamentalist Christians, who speak about being "born again" and who make exclusive claims on God's truth. Catholics, who have a different style of piety, often feel intimidated in these situations. Resolving these tensions requires that we have confidence in our own theology and spirituality. There are indeed a variety of religious experiences and many ways of encountering Almighty God. The norm for judging the authenticity of these experiences remains Jesus Christ revealed in the Scriptures and proclaimed in the church.

Catholics also experience certain tensions in encountering other religions. The great religious traditions of the world can challenge us to rethink our own understanding of the divine-human relationship and to reexamine our religious commitments. For example, the Muslims who accuse us of tritheism force us to rethink our understanding of God. The serenity achieved by Buddhist monks moves us to rediscover our own contemplative tradition.

Contemporary theology provides us with a framework for making interfaith encounters more fruitful. God wills the salvation of all people. Every human being is encompassed by God's grace and thus participates in a universal revelation. The world's great religious traditions are authentic vehicles of grace and instruments for spreading good in the world. For us Christians, Jesus Christ is the final prophet and the absolute savior. Our commitment to Christ as the norm should make us more open to the truth, goodness and beauty found in other religious traditions.

This theological perspective enables us to enter into interfaith dialogue with a sense of both confidence and openness. Today we are more aware that the cause of world peace can be furthered by effective dialogue which will transform the current tensions into mutually beneficial collaboration.

This book is based on the conviction that the tensions we experience in the church today can become more fruitful through theological reflection, improved dialogue and charitable cooperation. We must discover and celebrate deeper sources of unity which transcend our points of disagreement. Conflicting mindsets, theologies and strategies can be reconciled only by finding points of agreement which are more fundamental and more important. The key to making progress toward the ideal of unity in diversity is for all of us to deepen our commitment to Christ and the Gracious Mystery he reveals.

Chapter One

Dealing With Grievances and Dissent

---

1. Progressive Catholics and the World Church

Many progressive Catholics are expressing concern about the rigid, centralizing tendencies which seem to be growing in the Church. Middle-aged Catholics who have worked hard to free themselves from a legalistic training are especially sensitive to any suggestions of undoing the reforms of the Second Vatican Council. Sisters who treasure the freedom they now enjoy in their religious communities are deeply concerned about the efforts of the Roman Curia to impose inflexible patterns in life-style and governance.

Contemporary theologians who search for creative ways to make the Gospel relevant for our own times are disturbed by Vatican restrictions on Charles Curran, Hans Küng and others. Women who want to share fully their gifts and talents with the faith community are extremely frustrated with the negative responses of the papacy on the question of women's ordination and status in the Church. Pastors who

1

want their parishes to manifest the spirit of the Second Vatican Council have to contend with rigid reactions from the Roman Curia, such as the condemnation of the popular catechism *Christ Among Us.*

Progressives who hoped that the Council would unleash a whole series of reforms are now fearful that the trend is toward retrenchment rather than experimentation. Freedom-loving young people, who know the pre-Vatican II Church mostly through exaggerated horror stories, can hardly imagine living in a more conservative Church than the one they see today. As these examples make clear, a growing number of liberal Catholics are anxious because they sense the heavy hand of a new authoritarianism in the Church.

In search for perspective on this situation, I instinctively turn to Karl Rahner, the great German Jesuit theologian. In 1979 Rahner produced an often-quoted article entitled "Basic Theological Interpretation of the Second Vatican Council" (*Theological Investigations*, Vol. XX, p. 77 ff). Rahner placed the centralizing tendencies in the Church in the context of a Catholic community in process of becoming, for the first time, a "World Church." In this extremely influential article, Rahner makes clear his opposition to the Vatican tendency to strive for control over the whole Church. He insists, for example, that "the Roman congregations still have the mentality of a centralized bureaucracy which thinks it knows best what serves the kingdom of God and the salvation of souls throughout the world."

Rahner also sees, however, a larger historical process going on. The first-century Christian community passed through a momentous change when, under Paul's leadership, it moved from being a predominantly Jewish Church to being a Gentile Church. This decisive move involved significant changes, such as transferring the Sabbath from Saturday to Sunday and moving the center of Church life from Jerusalem to Rome. The Church today, in Rahner's opinion, is going through a transition of similar proportions. We are moving from being a Western Church to becoming, for the first time in history, a World Church.

In this new era, Christianity will gradually establish genuine roots in Asian, African and Latin cultures. The previous practice of exporting Western forms of Christianity from Europe and the United States will gradually be replaced by genuine evangelization. We can only begin to imagine the rich and intriguing shape of indigenous forms of an Asian and an African Christianity which fully reflect the uniqueness of these cultures. From this global perspective the Second Vatican Council appears not as the end or capstone of 19th- and 20th-century liberal movements, but as a tentative beginning of a *new era* in which the Church will gradually become a genuine worldwide community.

Rahner's analysis has many implications. The Church of the future will be even more pluralistic, manifesting many diverse expressions of the essential gospel message. Any thought of returning to Christendom or a monolithic Catholic culture will be exposed as an unrealistic attempt to buck the tide of history. It will be clear that one uniform Canon Law to control the diverse national Churches is no longer possible.

Indigenous liturgies reflecting local customs will take forms quite different from the standard Roman liturgy. This has already occurred in the Massai tribe in eastern Africa where the Eucharist is an all-day celebration and employs native dance forms.

In Rahner's World Church there will be pressure for the pope to voluntarily renounce power and to function as the spiritual leader of the federated Christian Church. Since this new stage in the history of the Church is just now beginning, it is difficult to even imagine the kind of changes which will be called for in a truly global Church.

If the scenario suggested by Rahner even approximates the future reality, then history is on the side of those Catholics who desire more freedom and decentralization. Pluralism will simply be a fact of life in a World Church which respects the distinctive characteristics of national and local cultures. Any attempt to impose a rigid, centralized control on national Churches will be seen as an anachronistic and futile effort to retard the inevitable formation of indigenous forms of Christian life.

This vision of the future Church may not ease the current pain of those Catholics who feel the weight of a new authoritarianism. It can, however, be a source of hope and inspiration for those who choose to continue the fight for a gospel-inspired freedom within the Church.

Rahner's scenario also suggests the importance of continuing to bring the distinctive experience of the Church in the United States into the general consciousness of the universal Church. Our particular understanding of religious liberty became an essential part of the teaching of the Second Vatican Council through the fine scholarly work of our outstanding theologian, John Courtney Murray, and the influence of the United States' bishops who pressed for acceptance of the religious liberty document. Our flourishing national Church has much more to offer the global Catholic community. The World Church Rahner envisions will welcome our distinctive experience and insights—and be enriched by them.

Catholics who wish to see Rahner's vision become reality must hold fast to the progressive advances already contained in the teachings of the Second Vatican Council. Greater liturgical diversity, more optimistic teachings on God's universal will to save all people, broader notions of revelation, and greater openness to the world's great religious traditions—these approaches and teachings have to become an integral part of the outlook of all Catholics so that the gains of Vatican II will not be lost. If Catholics make full use of the legitimate freedom already in place, then it will be harder for the Roman bureaucracy to reintroduce rigid control.

The very threat of a more rigid authoritarian spirit in the Church can be a catalyst to sharpen and refine the goals, convictions and methods of progressive Catholics. Prudence and balance ought to guide this effort. Freedom, for example, should always be discussed in the context of a sense of responsibility to the Church as a whole. Reformed liturgical celebrations should preserve and enhance a sense of Mystery. Contemporary theology should respect the Christian tradition and remain in clear judgment upon the demonic and destructive tendencies in our culture. Experimentation should be carried out responsibly. The quest for women's rights in the Church should allow for diversity of approaches and include methods calculated to influence open-minded leaders.

Liberals should not speak of discarding the institutional model of the Church but of balancing it with more communal models. Ecumenical dialogue and cooperation should reflect fidelity to the gospel of Jesus Christ and not give the impression of a search for the lowest common denominator. Criticism of the Church should be offered in a spirit of loyalty.

Modern approaches to the Scriptures should maintain a proper notion of inspiration. Talk of a universal revelation should include the conviction that Jesus Christ is indeed the Word of God and the final prophet. The emphasis on the steadfast love of a merciful God should not rule out a healthy sense of sin.

These suggestions reflect a solid theology which thinks more in terms of "both-and" than "either-or." They are also based on the pragmatic notion that one should not needlessly supply authoritarian critics with ammunition. Progressive Catholicism must be prudent if it is to continue to be a force for renewal in the global Church.

The anguish and fears of progressive Catholics are real and must be taken seriously. Rigid authoritarianism hurts human beings and often makes victims of those who have served the Church most generously and loyally. Those of us who believe in the liberal goals of responsible freedom and healthy pluralism must maintain a hopeful realism which includes a broad perspective on the future and a practical wisdom for living in the World Church.

2. A Liberating Church: The Real Answer to Critics

I talk to a number of people who are turned off by religion. Their litany of negative statements has become quite familiar:

- All they ever do in church is preach about money.
- The nuns crammed all the pious stuff down my throat.
- My parents forced their beliefs on me and I don't want any part of that now.
- Most churchgoers are hypocrites anyway.
- All religion does is make people feel guilty.
- I don't buy the superstitious doctrines and rituals anymore.
- The Churches have a lot of money while other people are starving.
- Priests are out of touch with the real world.
- I don't get much out of going to Mass.
- I am not comfortable with all the talk of hell and damnation.
- The Church's teachings on many moral questions, especially on sexual matters, do not make sense to me anymore.

How are we to respond to such a list of grievances? Even more important, how do we respond to the individuals who often reveal a deep disquiet when they make such statements?

One approach is to blame the dissidents for their moral failings. Some studies suggest that most Catholic young people who stop going to church do so because they have adopted a life-style, especially in the sexual area, which is at odds with what they perceive to be official Church teaching. Citing such studies, some critics claim that if the dissidents repented of their moral faults, they would recognize the value of religion and accept the Church.

This approach, however, is inadequate because it fails to deal honestly with the fundamental ambiguity of religion and the sinfulness of the Church itself. We will get a more complete picture of the problem—and the solution—by carefully examining our religious tradition in order to discern its strengths and weaknesses, its power to liberate as well as to enslave.

Certain themes developed by contemporary sociology, especially as interpreted by Christian thinkers such as Gregory Baum (*Religion and Alienation*) and Andrew Greeley (*The Catholic Myth*), offer a great deal of help in this discernment. The sociological perspective reminds us, for instance, that we are institutional creatures, necessarily involved in various organizations, systems and structures. Human beings create institutions, but these institutions then take on a life of their own with tremendous power to form the consciousness, shape the imagination and influence the behavior of individuals.

This reciprocal relationship is often mediated through symbols which influence us in hidden ways. For example, as citizens of the United States we are greatly affected by the important symbols of the American civil religion, such as the Constitution and the saintly founder, George Washington. Our sense of reality is shaped by these symbols, whether or not we recognize them as constituting a distinctive symbol system or way of life.

Based on this dialectical interaction between individuals and their institutions, sociologists insist that religion cannot be confined to private matters of the heart. It necessarily takes on structural forms. Thus religion is defined as a symbol system (including myths, creeds, rituals, doctrines and laws) which provides an interpretation of reality and which helps hold a culture together. This symbol system exists as an independent reality with a life of its own. Individuals are socialized into it. To grow up as a Catholic, therefore, is to drink in the centrality of the Eucharist and all this implies about the nature of God, the role of Christ and the structure of the Church.

As an institutional reality, religion involves a fundamental ambivalence. It can be a force for good or for evil; it can legitimate unjust situations or call for reform; it can promote superstition or liberate people for intelligent inquiry; it can foster prejudice or teach equality; it can help keep people in an infantile state or enable them to move toward maturity; it can enslave or liberate; it can encourage a narrow exclusivism or foster a healthy open-mindedness; it can cause neurotic guilt feelings or produce a healthy sense of creaturehood; it can cause suffering or work to reduce it.

In short, religion can diminish or promote the truly human. We can see this general principle exemplified in the way the symbol of the kingdom has functioned historically in Christianity.

Jesus began his ministry by proclaiming that the kingdom of God was at hand and that the time of repentance was *now*. He described this kingdom, or reign, of God through his parables. The kingdom is present where there is peace and justice, where harmony prevails and where suffering is combated.

A new sense of morality governs life in the kingdom. A person is to turn the other cheek, go the extra mile and even forgive enemies. The kingdom which becomes identified with the cause and person of Jesus is already here, but will be complete and perfect only at the endtime. Thus the image of the kingdom is at the center of the teaching of Jesus and has been used by Christians throughout history to understand human existence and to organize constructive behavior in the world.

But from the perspective of the human growth encouraged by the New Testament, this symbol of the kingdom has not always functioned in a positive way. Some have identified the kingdom Jesus preached with the Church and concluded that the Church is a perfect society which possesses all truth and a holy community which can do no wrong.

This distorted theology makes it impossible to speak honestly with those who feel they have suffered real harm from their participation in the Christian community. One is reduced to telling them to mend their ways and return to Holy Mother Church. This leaves those who feel injured by religion few options but to reject their religious heritage.

When Church and kingdom are identified, there is no room for admission that real harm may have been done on both sides of the conflict between person and institution. When the Church assumes an aura of perfection which ought to be reserved for the reign of God, there is little motivation to uncover hidden contradictions in the faith community and no compelling reason to make reforms. This is a far different image of Church than the Vatican II notion of a pilgrim people, a sinful community in need of reform, a *limited* sign of the kingdom.

Another misuse of the kingdom symbol is to equate it with heaven and, in effect, to deny that the kingdom is present and growing in our real world. This leads to an other-worldly piety which focuses on heaven and neglects the task of improving the human situation here and now. From this perspective, Christianity has everything to do with saving one's soul and nothing to do with fighting injustice or humanizing our world. It functions as a drug which dulls our human sensitivity to the sufferings which pervade the world. The disadvantaged are encouraged to put up with their lot, and any talk of liberation is reserved to political revolutionaries.

While admitting these destructive tendencies, it is also important to emphasize that the kingdom image can function positively and has done so historically. If the Church is indeed the sign of the kingdom, then it is vital that this sign be credible. The Church must honestly face the contradictions and sins which keep it from illuminating and fostering God's reign. All the members are coresponsible for improving the quality of life in the Church and making sure it reflects the values and teachings of Jesus. The kingdom image thus leads to a healthy self-criticism and an ongoing reform of the Church.

A proper understanding of the kingdom ideal can also lead to active involvement in the world on behalf of peace and justice. Christians know that God is fighting against evil in our world and that we are called to join in this crusade. The ideal of the kingdom can remind us of how humans ought to live. It can sharpen our awareness of the inequities built into the institutions of our world and move us to constructive action on behalf of the disadvantaged.

The truth is, the central teaching of Jesus about the reign of God need not dehumanize us. On the contrary, the kingdom ideal has an amazing power to reveal dehumanizing structures and tendencies in both the Church and the world and to promote healthy efforts to create more humane institutions and situations.

This analysis of the way the symbol of the kingdom mediates the relationship between individuals and the ideals of the institutional Church provides a framework for responding to critics. However, those who are turned off because the Church appears as a dehumanizing force will no doubt be more impressed with constructive actions than with abstract theories. We make our best case by actually functioning as faith communities which encourage personal development and work diligently for justice and peace.

3. Advice for a Returning Catholic

Dear Tom,

This is a response to your letter about returning to the Church. Seventeen years is a long time, and a great deal has happened to you and the Church during that period.

I will begin by commenting on some of your problems with the Church. Clearly the birth control encyclical, *Humanae Vitae,* was a major factor in your leaving the Church. Right now about 80 percent of the Catholics in the United States, including priests, agree with your position that the use of contraception in marriage can be the best moral option. In this regard it is important to note that Pope John Paul II has continued to insist on the official teaching found in *Humanae Vitae* and that our bishops have encouraged us to take seriously its outlook on the fruitfulness of married love. Nevertheless, surveys indicate that many Catholics are making their own decisions on this question and do so with an easy conscience.

I have to agree with some of your comments about divorce and remarriage. I also know of cases in which couples married 20 years with four children have gotten annulments. In fact, very few cases are turned down these days. On the other hand, it is not true that affluent individuals can simply buy annulments for thousands of dollars.

I do, however, concur with your main point: We are giving off double signals by granting so many annulments. If we got out of the annulment business completely, we could put more energy into preparing young people well for marriage and helping married couples enrich their relationships. This would provide a more consistent witness to the ideal of lifelong partnership based on fidelity and love. Unfortunately, it does not appear that you will see a major change in the annulment procedures in the near future.

You mentioned your fear of running into an authoritarian pastor. That is possible since there are still a couple of those left! The ideal is to affiliate with your local parish and work to improve it. It is no secret, however, that some Catholics shop around these days for a parish that they like and that meets their spiritual needs. I would rather have you do that than encounter unnecessary obstacles in returning to the Church.

You mentioned Confession. I certainly would advise you to choose your confessor carefully and not take a chance of running into a priest who is insensitive or forgets that the sacrament is primarily a proclamation of God's mercy. The great spiritual masters have generally advised a prudent selection of a spiritual guide, and that seems especially important in your case.

That you have continued to pray during all these years and that your image of God has developed significantly does not surprise me. I am glad you now perceive the One running this world as caring and trustworthy rather than as judgmental and harsh. I can understand the guilt feelings you felt those first few years and am glad they have subsided. My sense is that you have actually matured spiritually during this time and are ready to affiliate again with the Church on the basis of strength rather than weakness. God has mysterious ways of bringing good out of difficult situations.

What prompted your renewed interest in the Church is not really clear to me. My experience, guided by some of the current literature, tells me that individuals return for a number of reasons: the desire to rediscover roots and a clear value system (perhaps your current dissatisfaction with your job has something to do with it); the good example of significant people (your brother's perseverance despite all of his troubles could be a factor); or a special event which shakes up ordinary thinking (the birth of your grandson may well qualify).

But I am not sure that it is all that important to know why. A woman stopped in the other day to discuss her return to the Church. She had not gone to Mass for 30 years and claims she never thought much about it. One Saturday afternoon she was driving by a Catholic Church when Mass was being celebrated. For some unknown reason she stopped abruptly and went in. The setting and the ritual all seemed so different to her. She was confused, but she also felt a mysterious inner peace. She is now going to Mass regularly while trying to learn more about the changes in the Church.

Who can explain such happenings! It seems better to breathe a simple prayer of gratitude and get on with life.

You are also going to need some theological updating. Much of what is being said today by theologians corresponds with your own deep desire for self-fulfillment:

There is a source of our drive for a richer and deeper life which we call God. This God has given us gifts and talents and expects us to develop them for the sake of the common good.

Jesus Christ is for us the greatest example of the good life lived in response to God. He is the best that the human race has produced and is thus God personally present for us. He is both invitation and model for us in our search for healthy self-fulfillment.

At its best, the Church is a community which celebrates and facilitates personal growth and development. In the faith community we hope to find genuine support in our struggles and stimulating challenges to become our better selves. The local parish should be the place where we experience liberation and can live out a responsible freedom.

I know, sadly enough, that your experience with the Church in the past was not particularly liberating. You certainly did encounter your share of authoritarian priests, moralistic sisters and self-righteous parishioners. Many Church teachings did seem to contradict your experience and impede your development.

We both know that there are no utopian situations in life, but there is reasonable hope that this time around you can find a parish which better meets your needs. I know of parishes which are genuine faith communities with vibrant liturgies, effective religious education programs and constructive activities on behalf of peace and justice. They give me hope that more progress can be made in this direction if we work at it together with diligence and intelligence.

Wherever you end up, I expect you will find a greater sense of pluralism than you remember from the past. It is not hard to distinguish "progressives" who want more changes, "conservatives" who prefer the traditional ways, and "charismatics" who stress the gifts of the Holy Spirit.

You will also find a greater number of "selective Catholics" who have not left the Church but who hang pretty loose from the structure. They don't feel guilty about missing Mass and are not particularly interested in what the pope and bishops have to say. They are not angry with the Church; they simply take what they like and leave the rest go. This approach is a reality in today's Church, and I suspect you will have to come to terms with it.

You asked for a personal response. It bothers me that you felt the need to leave in the first place. All of us who comprise the Church must examine our conscience and ask forgiveness for the ways we have distorted the Body of Christ and made it less attractive to others.

I do not think of your return to the Church on the model of the Prodigal Son. You have clearly not lost your faith nor squandered your time and talents. My hope is that regular participation in the life of a local parish will now focus your energies, strengthen your values, reinforce your commitments and make you even more responsive to the person and message of Christ.

I welcome your return because the community has been impoverished by your absence. We need the specific contributions you have to make. You should reaffiliate as a full participant, not as a marginal person.

I recognize that you may have to go slowly and gradually test your reactions; but in the long run I hope you assume responsibility for your parish and become part of the solution rather than a mere critic of the problems. Personally, I am extremely pleased that you are moving in this direction and am praying that you receive both a warm welcome and the encouragement to use your valuable gifts for the benefit of the Church.

4. Anti-Catholic Bias: What Fuels Some Fundamentalist Critics

Dear Ken,

This letter is a follow-up to our recent conversation, which left me vaguely dissatisfied. It enables me to offer a more thoughtful response to your story, especially your recent drift away from the Catholic Church. My hope is that as you begin your junior year in college you will at least consider my interpretation of your religious journey, as well as my advice for future direction.

In my mind, your upbringing in a good Catholic home is a great resource for growth and not a neutral phase, as you see it. Your parents strike me as generous Christians who put their religion into practice through their involvement in the community and the parish. Obviously they are not perfect, but their participation in adult religious education programs indicates that they have tried to grow in their faith along the lines suggested by the Second Vatican Council.

As I see it, your years in the drug scene in high school not only got you in trouble but also reduced your self-confidence. Your low self-esteem carried over into your freshman year in college, contributing to your general lethargy and despondency.

Confused and insecure, you were a prime target for the aggressive proselytizing of your nondenominational Christian fellowship. My interpretation is that their "love bombing" approach made you feel better about yourself, and the warm fellowship of the group gave you a sense of security. By insisting that Christ has atoned for our sins once and for all by shedding his blood on the cross, they helped you feel forgiven and liberated from the residual guilt connected with your days in the drug culture. This surely was an important step forward in your spiritual development or, as you call it, your "walk with the Lord."

But it seems to me that your current walk also includes some dangerous pitfalls. What worries me most is the exclusive attitude you are picking up from your Christian fellowship. The suggestion that your good parents are not saved because they have not been "born again" is a clear distortion of the essence of the Good News. Historically, religious exclusivism has brought immense suffering into the world by fostering wars, crusades and inquisitions. Today we can discern its destructive influence in Northern Ireland and in the Middle East. Closer to home, it is causing painful rifts in families like yours.

The religious outlook you have embraced is not just one more diverse opinion on theological matters. It is a total package which has forced you into rejecting your own parents and part of your very self.

Do you understand how they feel when you insist that you became Christian for the first time last year? Not only do you deny your own existence as a Catholic Christian for 20 years, but you imply that Catholics are not really Christians, even if they lead good lives as your parents have done.

It does not surprise me that your nondenominational group forced you to make a choice between them and your Catholic heritage. At first it was fine to come to their Bible study and to attend Mass as well. When they were convinced that you were firmly in their camp, however, your shepherd issued the ultimatum to choose one or the other. Your decision at that point to drop out of the Catholic Church was certainly not surprising.

Let me comment again on your list of grievances against the Catholic religion. You claim that Catholics deny the unique mediatorship of Christ; discourage the reading of the Bible; worship Mary; recrucify Christ at Mass; confess sins to a priest and not to God; and emphasize nonbiblical doctrines such as purgatory. While you presented these objections as your considered judgment after a long period of study extending for six months, you and I both know they really came from the leaders of your fellowship and the anti-Catholic reading material they gave you. I have heard the same list of objections from numerous collegians, often expressed in virtually the same words.

Among certain segments of fundamentalist Christians, there exists a sharply-defined stereotypical package of anti-Catholic bias which accounts for these often-repeated objections. This outlook unfortunately obscures any realistic appraisal of contemporary Catholicism.

It is remarkable how totally opposed this biased package is to your own experience as a Catholic. You attended Mass regularly for years where all the prayers ended by affirming the unique mediatorship of Christ. Three selections from the Scriptures were read at every weekend Mass; and your parish regularly offered Bible study classes, many of which your parents attended. In your eighth-grade religion class, you were encouraged to read through one of the Gospels, searching for your favorite image of Jesus. Mary played almost no role in your parents' spirituality, and you were never even taught how to say the rosary. You never heard one word in homilies or classes about recrucifying Christ at Mass. The dominant message you heard about Confession is that it is a reminder of God's mercy. When your grandmother died, no one spoke about her going to purgatory.

The anti-Catholic talk you hear in your group is not even close to your own experience. This should tell you that something is wrong. I am waiting for you to really think for yourself and to trust your own experience in these matters.

As is the case with all religions, Catholicism has its strengths and weaknesses. Historically, we have known our share of distortions. For instance, you can find examples of Catholic piety which overplay Mary and thereby diminish the mediatorship of Christ. That, however, is not the official Church position, especially as enunciated by the Second Vatican Council; nor is it the common piety you have experienced in your home or parish. If you are going to reject your Catholic heritage, you should do so based on accurate perceptions of contemporary Church practices and teachings and not on an outdated stereotypical package kept alive by unenlightened fundamentalists.

Finally, I suggest you use your critical intelligence in examining not only your Catholic heritage but also your current fellowship. You might ponder these questions: Why do they feel a need to be so anti-Catholic? Why are they so reluctant to participate in ecumenical and interfaith dialogue? Do they indeed manifest religious exclusivity, as I have suggested? Do you find enough emphasis in their preaching on the social dimension of the gospel and the struggle for peace and justice? How are women treated in the fellowship, and do you agree with the notion that they should be subservient to men? Do some of the literal interpretations of the Bible make sense to you? For example, is creationism defensible in the light of modern science? Do you really agree with a biblical interpretation which leads to the conclusion that your parents are not saved?

It would be great if we could open up dialogue with the leaders and members of your fellowship on these questions and others of your choosing. I would hope that we could proceed on the basis of charity and mutual respect which befits Christians.

Ken, I have talked with many Catholics who, like you, have been attracted to exclusive fundamentalist groups. Some had troubled pasts, while others were blessed with a smoother journey. For the most part, these students have struck me as good and sensitive persons. Generally, they have been serious about religious matters but unfortunately limited by a narrow base of experience, as well as by inadequate biblical and theological knowledge. I feel the same way about you.

My faith tells me you remain in God's gracious love, even if your sincere walk takes you further away from the Catholic Church. I hope my comments reflect my respect for you and the seriousness of your spiritual quest.

I am convinced, on the other hand, that you are proceeding on your religious journey with incorrect perceptions and inadequate knowledge. My fear is that you will fall into an increasingly rigid exclusivism which will seriously harm you, your family and your ability to do good in the world. My hope is that you will take my advice to heart by prayerfully and intelligently reexamining your current walk with the Lord.

5. *In Vitro*: Vatican Wisdom and Legitimate Dissent

Sue and Jack are one of an estimated nine million infertile couples in the United States. They are upset by the strict prohibitions against artificial means of achieving pregnancy contained in the 1987 Vatican instruction on human life and procreation. (See "Instruction on Respect for Human Life in Its Origin and on the Dignity of Procreation," issued by Cardinal Joseph Ratzinger, head of the Congregation for the Doctrine of the Faith.)

Although they are good practicing Catholics, Sue and Jack intend to keep pursuing in vitro fertilization, the medical procedure suggested by their doctor in order to conceive a child. Sue insists that the Church leaders who decided that all artificial means of achieving pregnancy are wrong do not appreciate the anguish, the self-doubts and the deep desires for a child experienced by infertile couples.

Important moral theologians have also publicly expressed their reservations about the Vatican's total ban on artificial fertilization methods for married couples. For example, Richard McCormick, S.J., the highly-respected expert on bioethical questions, has sharply criticized the argumentation employed by the Vatican instruction in its rejection of in vitro fertilization and embryo transfer—the so-called "simple case" in which the wife's egg is fertilized by her husband's sperm in laboratory vessels and then placed in her womb.

This technique has produced more than 2,000 successful pregnancies since Louise Brown, the first in vitro baby, was born in England in 1978. It has gained rather wide, if cautious, acceptance among ethicists, including respected Catholic moral theologians.

The Vatican instruction argues that there is an inseparable connection between the unitive and procreative meanings of the conjugal act. In other words, the act of intercourse by its very nature and structure must express both the love of the spouses and, at the same time, their openness to the gift of new life. Just as *artificial contraception* is immoral because it breaks this intimate connection between the two meanings of the conjugal act by allowing the expression of love without the possibility of conception, so *artificial fertilization* is morally wrong because it breaks the bond by desiring procreation apart from the loving act of intercourse.

The instruction clearly states that "the procreation of a person must be the fruit and result of married love." The document specifies the meaning of this statement when it insists that children conceived through medical techniques are reduced to an object of scientific technology and are not really the fruit of their parents' love.

McCormick responds to this particular argument by noting that sexual intercourse is not the only way for married couples to express their love. The suggestion that infertile couples who utilize artificial insemination or in vitro fertilization are acting in a selfish or unloving way is gratuitous at best. It could be argued, on the contrary, that couples who go through the complicated and discomforting medical procedures are manifesting a very generous spirit desirous of making love fruitful.

Although the Vatican spent 20 months preparing this instruction, critics have noted that it fails to tap the experience of infertile couples or to engage the arguments of liberal theologians. Furthermore, critics argue, the document reflects a questionable understanding of the natural law—one which ultimately rests on the biological structure of the physical act of sexual intercourse.

This is the same type of argument which the Vatican employed in rejecting artificial birth control. It has not been persuasive for most Christians, including many theologians, who assess the morality of particular sexual and procreative actions by examining the whole context of loving, interpersonal relationships and not just by noting the physical nature of intercourse.

Many people accept the notion that conjugal acts should, ideally, combine mutual love with openness to life. But they have trouble seeing how specific actions involving artificial fertilization are necessarily destructive of this ideal of fruitful love.

Catholics who find the arguments against artificial fertilization techniques for married couples to be less than compelling must avoid the temptation to write off the whole instruction as an authoritarian pronouncement issued by uninformed Vatican officials. This would be extremely unfortunate, especially since the document does reflect a broad knowledge of medical advances and suggests ethical considerations which are crucial for the expanding debate on these procreative technologies.

When the instruction was first published, influential secular sources immediately recognized its importance. *The New York Times*, for instance, gave it extensive coverage, publishing the entire text, including the footnotes. Appearing on NBC's *Meet the Press*, then-Senator Albert Gore welcomed the document, noting that it could help shape the public debate on the complex issues raised by the new fertilization techniques.

The Vatican instruction is valuable precisely because it insists that ethical considerations must play a role in dealing with the new reproductive technology. Not everything which is scientifically possible is morally acceptable. Proper limits must be set and we need wide-ranging discussions in order to reach public consensus on where to draw these lines.

The Vatican document reminds us that larger social values must be considered in setting these limits and evaluating the morality of the new methods. The understandable desire of infertile couples like Sue and Jack for a child, loving and anguished as this longing may be, cannot be the only consideration in a comprehensive moral evaluation. We must also consider the common good, including the effects on the institution of marriage and on other persons involved.

This larger perspective raises serious objections to the third-party solutions to infertility problems which involve donors and surrogates. Although the instruction bases its absolute prohibition against the use of donor sperm and eggs, as well as surrogate mothers, on the unity of marriage and the rights of the child, it also suggests that we consider the social and institutional values involved.

Richard McCormick and other theologians have helped specify these societal values. McCormick's probing analysis leads to serious questions: Will the widespread use of surrogate mothers, for example, involve exploitation of poor women? Will it cause psychological damage to other women like Mary Beth Whitehead, who cannot give up their children because of the natural bonding that has occurred? Will surrogates feel used or be hurt by participating in actions traditionally frowned upon by society—that is, conceiving a baby apart from a loving commitment and failing to raise the child once born?

Will marriage partners feel threatened by the psychological presence of the third-party donor which continually reminds them of their own inability to produce a child? How will the self-identity of children be affected by having three parents—or even five parents (donors for sperm and egg, a surrogate mother, and a couple raising the child)? What effect will the widespread use of third parties have on the stability of the institution of marriage, which is so essential to a healthy society?

What are the long-range consequences for the scientific community and the medical profession when they are called upon to produce children upon request or to design a particular type of child with certain desirable characteristics? What fundamental changes occur in human consciousness when scientific experts possess the capability of genetically engineering coming generations?

We do not have sufficient data on these and other questions involving institutional and societal values. Simply to ask these questions, however, suggests that potential risks are involved which must be considered in assessing the morality of the new procreative technology. The Vatican instruction performs a valuable service by fostering and focusing continued debate on these crucial questions. As technological procedures advance and the questions become even more complicated, we surely need the kind of wisdom found in our Judeo-Christian heritage.

This analysis suggests that disagreements with official Church teachings should be prayerfully and thoughtfully considered. Blanket rejections are seldom wise or prudent. Even controversial Church statements often contain general principles and particular insights which dissenting members ought to consider for their own benefit.

6. Women's Ordination and the Importance of Dissent

Dissent in the Catholic Church today takes many forms. Some conservative Catholics, for example, disagree with the bishops' pastoral letter on the economy, while many liberals reject the papal teaching on birth control. The controversial issue of women's ordination to the priesthood provides a focus for examining the place of dissent in the Church.

In 1976 the Sacred Congregation for the Doctrine of the Faith published, with the approval of Pope Paul VI, "A Declaration on the Question of the Admission of Women to the Ministerial Priesthood." This statement declared that women could not be ordained priests because Jesus intended to exclude women from official public ministry for all times and under all sociological conditions. This official teaching of the Roman authorities was meant to close the matter and end public debate.

Now, many years later, the issue is more alive than ever, and dissent from the official teaching is growing. Opposition is evident among many groups and individuals: ordinary people who are offended by this seeming denial of fundamental human rights; priests who increasingly feel burdened by the shortage of ordained ministers; sisters who are frustrated by their dependence on an all-male priesthood; pastoral associates who are forced to bring in priests from the outside to celebrate parish Masses; dedicated but frustrated persons who have all but left the Church over this issue; and, finally, women who remain in the Church but also celebrate their own feminist liturgies.

The Vatican effort to quell dissent on this issue has obviously not worked. Instead, it has helped to produce a major crisis which threatens to grow in scope and intensity.

In searching for perspective on this issue, we should recall that our contemporary American culture fosters precisely this kind of dissent. Our democratic spirit prompts us to celebrate freedom and to demand that human rights be respected. Institutions are suspect and their policies are routinely challenged. The mass media provide a forum for dissent and consciousness-raising. Dissenters such as Mohandas Gandhi and Martin Luther King, Jr., take on heroic proportions in the minds of many.

The feminist movement participates in the energy generated by these modern ideals of freedom and equality. In our pluralistic world, Church leaders cannot effectively prohibit dissent by issuing a decree—especially on a volatile issue such as women's ordination.

Historically, dissent has always existed in the Church and has often enriched its life. Paul withstood Peter to his face and helped to create a more open attitude toward Gentile converts (see Galatians 2:11-14). Aquinas created a magnificent theological system by employing the Aristotelian thought previously forbidden by various popes. In our own time, John Courtney Murray, S.J., opposed the rigid official position on religious liberty and thus prepared the way for the more open teaching of the Second Vatican Council. Without minimizing the pain experienced by many today, we can interpret the drive for women's rights in the Church as one more step in a long process of realizing the implications of the inclusive love lived and taught by Jesus of Nazareth.

Theology provides us with further guidance on this question of dissent. We human beings are obliged to be responsible dissenters since we are called by God not simply to conform to institutional standards, but to respond freely to the divine summons which echoes in our hearts. As responsible social creatures, we must be concerned about those who suffer from institutional discrimination. Our dedication to Christ is lived out in a Church which has made mistakes in the past and which is committed to continuous reform in the light of the gospel.

It is important to remember that the Church, while remaining faithful to the essentials of the apostolic tradition, has always been pluralistic in theology, liturgy and spirituality. We find a particularly striking example of this pluralism early in the seventh century in an exchange between Pope Gregory the Great and Augustine of Canterbury, who was embarking on a missionary journey to England. On the question of liturgical adaptation, the Pope advised Augustine to examine practices in Rome, Gaul and other Churches and employ the ones which best fit the spirit of the people. Unfortunately, such an open attitude does not always prevail in the contemporary Church.

Since the First Vatican Council in 1870, the Church has made the explicit distinction between *dogma* and *doctrine*.

Dogmas are proposed with fullest solemnity as part of God's revelation. Doctrines are officially taught by the magisterium but are not considered to be infallible. Thus we can distinguish the unchanging dogmatic teaching on Christ as true God and true man from the doctrine (or official teaching) on birth control which is, at least in principle, subject to change.

Of course there is no complete official list of Church dogmas, and so there are disputes about whether particular teachings are dogmatic or doctrinal. And we must also recall that the Second Vatican Council called for religious obedience of will and intellect to Church *doctrines*. This implies that individuals must try to understand and accept particular doctrines, but it also recognizes that individuals may not be able to achieve an honest assent. Church leaders have an obligation to present good arguments for their teachings and to respect the consciences of those who cannot accept a particular doctrine.

Applying these theological principles to the official teaching on women's ordination, we see that dissent is possible in principle because this teaching is commonly understood as a doctrine and not a dogma. Influential theologians, including Karl Rahner, who have carefully studied the question, have indeed expressed disagreement with the main arguments of the Vatican declaration, which contend that Jesus intended to exclude women forever by choosing all males as apostles.

The dissenters argue that, given the patriarchal society of the time, it was impossible for Jesus to choose women as leaders or for women to function as official presiders at the Eucharist in the early Church. Furthermore, the dissenters ask how we can exclude women in the public proclamation of the gospel when Jesus himself commissioned women to take the joyful news of the resurrection to the apostles (see Luke 24:1-12). Given these considerations, Karl Rahner has insisted that the burden of proof is on those who adopt a rigid position, and that the Vatican has failed to offer persuasive arguments for this exclusionary policy.

Many sincere Catholics, without knowing all the intricate theological arguments, sense that the exclusion of women is opposed to the general thrust of the inclusive teaching of Jesus. They find the argument that women cannot be priests because they do not conform physically to the maleness of Jesus to be ludicrous. They are convinced that the Catholic community will be enriched by admitting women to full participation in the Church. (This point becomes more credible when combined with a realistic rejection of the utopian illusion that the ordination of women will suddenly usher in the kingdom.)

One of the strongest arguments advanced in favor of women's ordination is that the Eucharist must be preserved as the great sign and cause of unity. As it now stands, there is a growing danger that the Eucharist will actually be a cause of disunity since a significant number of women feel estranged from Masses always led by men. Furthermore, the declining number of priests in the United States means that more and more Catholics will be deprived of the opportunity to participate regularly in Mass.

Ordaining women would quickly solve this problem. It would also overcome the estrangement experienced by some women and enrich the Church with diverse charisms of leadership. A vital faith community empowers all members to use their gifts for building up the body of Christ.

At times, honest dissent is not merely permitted but demanded for the healthy development of the Church. A growing number of Catholics today feel an obligation to raise their voices in favor of women's rights so that the Church will become a more credible sign and effective instrument of the kingdom.

7. The Curran Affair: Authoritarian Spirit at Work

The "Curran affair" has already become an important part of the history of the Church in the United States. For many, it symbolizes the whole question of dissent in the Church.

But dissent is not merely a theological issue. It involves human beings with personalities and feelings who struggle with serious questions of conscience. Thus it seems important to recall not only the issues but also the man, Charles Curran, who has personally suffered from his dismissal from his cherished teaching position at The Catholic University as well as the refusal of other Catholic institutions to hire him.

The dispute centered on a conflict of views represented by Father Curran, then professor of moral theology at The Catholic University in Washington, D.C., and Cardinal Joseph Ratzinger, head of the Congregation for the Doctrine of the Faith. The publication of their correspondence (see *Origins,* March 26, 1986) clarified the essence of their respective positions.

The Cardinal saw the issue in terms of authority structures and the danger of scandal. Rome simply could not tolerate a theologian publicly teaching at The Catholic University, in the name of the Church, while denying official Church positions on such important issues as sexual morality and respect for life.

For Curran the main question was the right of dissent within the Church. His defense rested on these points: he has never denied an infallible Church dogma and has always treated official teaching with respect. Although he publicly dissented from some elements of noninfallible authoritative Church teaching, he did so prudently and legitimately. Curran cited Karl Rahner and Bernard Haring, among others, who hold that, for good reasons, a Catholic can dissent from official teaching. He also noted that the Catholic bishops of the United States have recognized the right of dissent as long as the reasons are well-founded and the dissent is carried out with respect for the magisterium and without giving scandal.

Curran constantly pushed Cardinal Ratzinger to declare where the Congregation stood on the question of public dissent. Did they really want to say that obedient silence is the only possible response for a theologian who, after prayer and study, cannot personally accept a particular doctrine? Part of Curran's defense was to recall that the Church has officially changed its teachings on important issues, such as religious liberty, in part because dissenting theologians have been able to convince others of their positions.

While pressing his point on public dissent, Curran also addressed the individual disputed points. In general, he tried to show that he had taken the official positions seriously and that other theologians supported his dissenting views. Throughout the whole seven-year controversy, he emphasized his respect for the Catholic tradition, his continuing fidelity to the Church and his willingness to seek a compromise.

During and after the controversy, Curran received strong support from theologians in the United States. Some who do not agree with him on all the particular moral issues still accept his general position on dissent in the Church.

Richard McCormick, S.J., has often insisted that dissent is the real issue in the controversy. He also points out that the Congregation neither clarified its position nor faced the ramifications of a rigid stance which would effectively rule out all dissent.

Many theologians think that Curran mounted a coherent and persuasive defense. Even those who were not convinced by his arguments generally praised him for his personal integrity.

My own position on the issue is no doubt affected by my positive perception of Charles Curran the man and by his immense efforts to popularize the renewal of moral theology. In my experience, he has been exceedingly generous in sharing his time and expertise.

I recall a phone conversation to him in Washington when he patiently summarized for me the latest debates on the peace pastoral so that I could be well prepared for an important lecture. There was a long and intense discussion in a restaurant in Dayton, Ohio, when he clarified for me his general approach to moral decision-making.

I have especially vivid memories of a lecture he gave around 1963 at the University of Colorado at Boulder. Drawing on a long tradition, he pointed out that the radical ethical demands of Jesus, as recorded in the New Testament, are best understood as moral ideals which call us to ever greater efforts, rather than as moral norms which admit no exceptions and bind in all circumstances. For example, he interprets the absolute prohibition against divorce in Mark's Gospel (19:9) as a call to strive for lifelong fidelity within a stable marriage. It is not an absolute law binding in every situation, as is clear from the exception for immorality already granted in Matthew's Gospel (19:9).

This notion of New Testament moral *ideals* puts the emphasis on the continuing effort to respond to a call which always invites a more generous love. These ideals help to avoid both a smug complacency and a neurotic guilt. It sets up a healthy tension between accepting who we are and striving to become our better selves in response to God's call.

This insight into moral ideals gleaned from Curran many years ago has guided my pastoral practice ever since. It has also provided me with a key for understanding his particular positions disputed by Cardinal Ratzinger.

On the questions of sexual morality, for example, Curran stresses the generous and faithful love which should exist between a woman and a man committed to each other in a lifelong marriage partnership. This is the ideal which sexual expression should strive to represent. In the real world, however, this ideal is not easily achieved. It runs up against obstacles which are a combination of circumstances beyond our control and free decisions already made in the past.

From this perspective, Curran admits that masturbation falls short of the full meaning of human sexuality. But at the same time, he denies that it should generally be thought of in the category of mortal sin. Individual acts are usually not very significant, he claims, and long-standing habits are better understood in psychological terms as pointing to deeper problems.

On the question of premarital sex, Curran insists that intercourse achieves its full meaning only within the commitment of marriage. He does believe, however, that there are very rare and comparatively few situations in which intercourse before marriage could be justified. An example might be if two people in love and committed to a permanent relationship are forced by external circumstances to postpone their marriage.

Elements of Curran's position are clearly at odds with official Church teaching. At the same time, however, we should note that many other theologians hold similar positions and that some Catholic moralists are more radical than Curran.

The removal of Charles Curran from his position at The Catholic University has produced many destructive consequences. First of all, an injustice has been inflicted on an admired and respected man described by his own bishop as an exemplary priest "deeply committed to the spiritual life." The injustice involved becomes more apparent when we recall that other theologians who hold similar views have not been investigated or punished.

Second, the Curia in its treatment of Curran has effectively denied the long-standing tradition of legitimate dissent from noninfallible doctrines. This unprecedented effort to suppress all such dissent has tended to stifle theological inquiry and creativity and to alienate creative thinkers from the Church as a whole. Reactionary elements in the Church have acquired new ammunition in their battle against liberal theological trends.

Third, we are now in greater danger of returning to more repressive approaches to sexuality. Many teachers and writers are now leery of expressing Curran's line of thought which admits of exceptions and emphasizes gradual growth toward full maturity. The charge that the Church refuses to deal honestly with the complex problems surrounding human sexuality has unfortunately been intensified.

Fourth, the action of the Curia has made it harder for Catholics in the United States to maintain that our institutions of higher education are genuine academic communities devoted to the pursuit of truth. We are now more open to the charge that they are simply proselytizing agents which repeat the party line of the Church hierarchy.

Fifth, the dismissal of Charles Curran signals a serious defeat for the renewal promised by Vatican II and for the struggle to find our own distinctive American voice. Although the Curran affair was far removed from the daily concerns of the average Catholic, I believe that it continues to have serious implications for the life of the Church in our country. A good man has suffered unjustly and the cause of progressive renewal has been damaged.

I think it is important for all segments of the Catholic community—including bishops, priests and laity who value freedom and treasure the distinctive characteristics of the Church in the United States—to retain a sense of outrage over the case and a sense of compassion for the man. Tomorrow the authoritarian spirit may touch closer to home.

8. A Proper Attitude Toward the Magisterium

The issue of dissent in the Church raises the question of the proper role of the magisterium, or official teaching office, within the Catholic community. Since the Second Vatican Council, many people have become more aware of the importance and complexity of this topic through the media coverage given to the disagreements between the Vatican and well-known theologians. These cases have raised difficult theological questions about the respective roles of bishops and theologians. The topic is important not just for theologians, however, but for all members of the Church.

As Catholics we live in a structured faith community with an official teaching authority. The frequent exercise of this teaching role through conciliar documents, doctrinal pronouncements, papal encyclicals and pastoral letters demands that we examine our attitudes toward the magisterium.

Without going into all the theological questions involved, I offer two major points for consideration: (1) The official teaching office in the Church is, ideally, a safeguard against the distortions of our own subjective outlook; (2) We must keep the magisterium in a proper perspective.

The harsh truth is that we have an immense capacity to fool ourselves. Rationalizations are easy to manufacture. We often think that our limited perspective is wider than it really is. It seems natural to think that our insights are more significant than those of other people. Our passions can cloud our reason and our needs can determine our perceptions.

The culture in which we live presents another set of problems. It shapes our consciousness to a greater degree than we usually want to admit. It becomes hard to distinguish which meanings and values are given to us by our American way of life and which come from our Christian faith.

Our capacity to distort extends to our appropriation of our faith. We can easily interpret the moral teachings of Christianity in a selective way and apply them in a self-serving fashion. It is possible to reject particular doctrines without sufficient thought and to interpret others according to our whims and interests.

Once we develop a healthy fear of our own illusions, then the need for a hierarchically-structured community becomes more evident. The magisterium, functioning as the official interpreter of the faith of the Christian community, provides a safeguard against the distortions of our own subjective outlook. It has the responsibility to set the limits of orthodoxy, to hand on the complete Christian message, to guard its purity and to confront people with the objective fact of the teachings of Jesus.

To do this effectively, Church leaders must have the power to state propositions which reflect the essence of the faith of the community as a whole. This power extends to the proclamation of official dogmas which infallibly reflect the Church's authentic understanding and essential union with the Lord. This is the case even when we consider the historical, cultural and linguistic limitations of these infallible propositions.

Someone has to be working to preserve the integrity of the Christian message and that job falls to the pope and bishops. In carrying out this task, they provide us with a challenge to our superficial perceptions and restricted outlooks.

Some people may think, for example, that the doctrine of the Assumption is irrelevant and that its infallible proclamation in 1950 was a mistake. But if these persons take this doctrine seriously and at least stay open to its potential meaning, they may eventually discover that the teaching about Mary has a message for all of us, including important insights on our common destiny, the significance of the human body and a proper context for discussing sexuality. These insights are especially important in a culture which has difficulty achieving a healthy integration of spirituality and sexuality.

The magisterium more often challenges our narrowness and superficiality through authoritative teaching which is reformable and not intended to be infallible. A prime example is the social teaching of the Church found in the modern papal encyclicals, such John XXIII's *Pacem in Terris* and John Paul II's *Centesimus Annus*. They serve as a powerful judgment upon the arrogant nationalism and the excessive consumerism which is so prevalent in our culture. These documents are used as a basis for discussion by scholars interested in creating a better world order. Most Catholics, unfortunately, have not yet caught up with the global vision and the sense of national interdependence taught by these encyclicals.

The social teaching propounded by Church leadership in this century has generally been progressive, and we would be impoverished without it. It remains a serious challenge to our personal viewpoints and our national policies. Even though this body of social teaching is not as well known as it should be, it still reminds us of the potential good involved in having authoritative teaching which expands our vision and calls us to responsible action.

While insisting on the essential, positive role of the official teachers in the Church, we must, however, keep the magisterium in a proper perspective. The pope and bishops alone do not constitute the Church. All of us who are baptized and profess the Lordship of Jesus make up the Church. Leaders in the Christian community are not to lord it over others but rather are to serve the other members, orchestrating their talents and gifts.

The magisterium should not function independently of the whole community; on the contrary, the pope and bishops should be in touch with the real problems of the people and should proclaim the gospel values from within the common human adventure. Dogmatic statements remain culturally, historically and linguistically conditioned, and even infallible statements can be improved, reinterpreted, restated and balanced. Historically it is clear that there is a development in the Church's self-understanding and that some official positions have been changed. For example, the positive teaching of Vatican II on salvation outside the Church clearly goes beyond previous restrictive views.

We need a theology of error which enables us to understand such developments and prepares us to admit mistakes without collapsing into a defensive position. There is a proper dissent in the Church. Conscience sometimes demands that we go against official statements of the leadership. Dissent from *Humanae Vitae* (the papal encyclical on birth control) by bishops, theologians and married couples is a clear example of individuals following their consciences rather than slavishly adhering to an official pronouncement. Church laws promulgated by the hierarchy are not absolutes but guidelines and directives facilitating Christian behavior. It is helpful to recall the traditional virtue of *epikeia* which guides one in knowing when and how to disregard or break particular laws because of extenuating circumstances.

Karl Rahner has suggested that in the future the magisterium will have to learn how to function effectively in a pluralistic world. This may mean giving more latitude to theologians to hammer out disputes among themselves, while recognizing the limitations of "Roman theology" in judging other theological systems. Effective leadership may also require that the magisterium avoid the formulation of new dogmas, allow for even more liturgical diversity and permit variations in Church laws in diverse cultural settings.

We can see the proper role of the magisterium more clearly by placing it in the larger framework of God's call to each individual and in the broader understanding of the Church as the whole people of God. From this perspective the official teaching office appears as an important check on our own self-centeredness and a valuable source of wisdom and guidance.

9. Matthew Fox: Healing Words That Can't Be Silenced

For the Dominican priest Matthew Fox, the year of Church-imposed silence ended in 1989. Since he is continuing to speak publicly, it is useful to reflect on his thought and influence.

Before beginning his year of silence, during which he was forbidden to teach, preach or lecture by order of Cardinal Ratzinger's Congregation for the Doctrine of the Faith, Father Fox publicly stated his side of the controversy. He accused the Vatican of "a new fundamentalist zeal" which leads to silencing creative thinkers and creating a climate of intimidation among theologians.

His own summary of the charges against him included: emphasizing original blessing instead of original sin, not condemning homosexuality, referring to God as Father and Mother, and being a "fervent feminist." Fox did not deny these charges, but defended himself by locating his own position within the broader context of a "creation spirituality" which, he says, is the "oldest tradition in the Bible." It was taught by the prophets, epitomized by Jesus and developed by the great medieval mystics such as Meister Eckhart and Julian of Norwich. Fox claimed at the time that "hundreds of thousands" worldwide ardently supported his movement,

25,000 of whom were members of his Friends of Creation Spirituality.

Fox's creation spirituality believes that passion is a blessing, not a curse, that beauty is more important than self-denial and that creativity should be emphasized more than obedience. It contends that "humans are essentially divine" and that the goals of the spiritual life are "compassion, justice and celebration." Creation spirituality is especially needed today because of the environmental crisis and the destructive dualism fostered by our patriarchal society. Fox concluded his statement with a plea for support, encouraging people to learn more about creation spirituality and to speak out in his defense.

The silencing of Fox can be seen in retrospect as a destructive action from many viewpoints. It failed to respect his dignity as a member of the Church, especially since this penalty was imposed without a formal hearing or an opportunity to respond to charges. It contributed to an atmosphere of fear in the world of Catholic scholarship which threatens the creative work of theologians. It angered and alienated many people who have experienced personal liberation through their encounter with creation spirituality. Even from the Vatican perspective, this oppressive action was counterproductive since it greatly increased Fox's visibility and expanded the market for his works.

Theologians, while decrying the Vatican action, have themselves been strangely silent about the content of Fox's works. There are very few serious theological critiques of his major works *Original Blessing* (1983) and *The Coming of the Cosmic Christ* (1988).

But some aspects of Fox's thought deserve criticism. For example, his characterization of the negative sin-redemption tradition represented by Augustine and the positive creation-centered tradition epitomized by Meister Eckhart does seem simplistic and one-sided.

A clever critic could begin by asking whether Augustine or Eckhart wrote these lines: "to be empty of all created things is to be full of God, and to be full of created things is to be empty of God"; "No one can accept fleshly and bodily consolations without spiritual damage"; "the sooner a man shuns what is created, the sooner will the creator come to him." When the answer is given that these are the words not of Augustine but of Eckhart (see "On Detachment"), questions begin to arise about Fox's delineation and characterization of two sharply-distinguished traditions. Further questions would arise by noting how crucial the theme of detachment is throughout Eckhart's writings and how much he is influenced by Augustine.

To concentrate on such theological objections, however, is to miss the real nature and significance of Fox's original contributions. He writes not as a systematic theologian but as a spiritual theologian who is interested in promoting full human development. He functions as a prophet who is passionate in denouncing the patterns of destruction in the contemporary world. He is a guru or a spiritual director who enables individuals to sense and tap the liberating power of the Spirit. He is a teacher who facilitates creativity in others by searching for wisdom in the world religions, especially the Judeo-Christian tradition. We will get more out of his writings by thinking of them as poetic commentaries by a passionate, imaginative spiritual director, rather than as systematic expositions by a traditional theologian.

Matthew Fox has made an impact because he has articulated genuine concerns and touched deep hurts. He recognized before many religious thinkers that we are indeed facing an ecological crisis. He has, moreover, been able to alert others to the problem by using symbolic language and religious categories. "Mother Earth is dying," he says, but the "Cosmic Christ," who is the centerpoint of the whole creation, can energize us and guide us in saving our mother.

Fox's sensitive spirit has enabled him to empathize with many people suffering from wounds of various types. He has articulated, for example, the pain of individuals who feel repressed by a heavy moralistic religious training. For the most part, these people do not care if Fox has properly interpreted Augustine's role in creating such a repressive atmosphere. All they know is that along the way they have picked up negative attitudes about sin and guilt which impede their personal growth. It is liberating to have someone identify the problems and suggest that there are more positive resources available in the Christian tradition.

Fox is also attuned to the destructive consequences of dualistic thinking which creates sharp divisions and hierarchies of power between various realities, such as soul and body, men and women, humans and nature, grace and nature. His writings, which attack dualism as the "sin behind all sins," often strike responsive chords with those who feel estranged and oppressed.

Not only does Fox give voice to pain and alienation, he also retrieves from the religious tradition helpful ideas for developing a more positive and healing approach to life. To counter the heavy Augustinian emphasis on original sin, Fox insists on the primacy of "original blessing" based on the continuous creative power of God's Word. He finds this positive approach in the biblical notion of the essential goodness of creation, in the Eastern Fathers' teaching that human beings are divinized, and in the medieval mystics' ecstatic delight in the closeness and beauty of God.

By stressing original blessing, we learn to delight in God's marvelous creation, to savor pleasure as an important path to God, and to appreciate sexuality as a beautiful, energizing gift from the Source of all blessings. If the creation is an original blessing for us, then we have a responsibility to be constructive citizens of the universe and prudent caretakers of the earth. We must learn to build the earth into a community of love by establishing patterns of justice to replace systems of oppression.

For Fox, "original blessing" is an encompassing category which directs our attention to the beauty of creation and the essential goodness of human nature. It encourages us to befriend the created world and to face the dark forces with confidence in the power of divine grace. It promotes the development of our potential in order to be more effective cocreators of the world and more compassionate people devoted to healing wounds and establishing justice.

In response to the problem of dualism, Fox gathers diverse notions from the Judeo-Christian tradition around the image of the Cosmic Christ. Borrowing a phrase, he suggests that Christ is "the pattern that connects" the apparent dualism between heaven and earth, past and future, grace and nature, soul and body, divinity and humanity.

The Cosmic Christ is the clue to the intelligible structure of reality, the harmonizing force which unifies the universe, the Word who brings all things to a final fulfillment. The risen Lord completes the work of the historical Jesus who challenged the artificial barriers between rich and poor, men and women, slave and free, Jew and Greek. The Cosmic Christ brings coherence into our lives by giving us hope that the chaos of division can be overcome and transformed into an enriching unity in diversity.

We do not have to agree with Fox's total analysis or all of his applications to appreciate the power of the Cosmic Christ image to help us overcome the sense of estrangement which is built into modern life. Healing words and integrating symbols which have liberated so many cannot finally be silenced.

10. A Perspective
for Disgruntled Parishioners

Dear Rita,

Your letter is disturbing. It saddens me to think of good Catholics like you feeling so stifled. It is hard for me to imagine a parish without lay distributors of Communion or women lectors. I am not aware of many situations like that in our part of the country.

Your efforts to talk to the pastor are certainly laudable, but he evidently has trouble incorporating your ideas into his own vision of parish life. I agree that you are working out of different models of the Church. It seems you really did master the material in the ecclesiology course taken from *Models of the Church* and *A Church to Believe In* by Avery Dulles. It pleases me to know that former students are making practical use of theology learned in the classroom.

Without knowing more about your actual situation, it is difficult to offer much practical advice. Some theological perspectives, however, might help you solidify your own thinking.
Since the time when you were in my class, another model of the Church has become more prominent: the local community of faith as the sacrament of the Spirit. I think it can provide some useful perspectives for your situation. To appreciate this model, it is important to recall the role of the Spirit in the drama of salvation.

Unfortunately, our theology of the Holy Spirit has not been very well developed in the Western Church. Nevertheless, we can draw on fairly recent books, such as Yves Congar's three-volume work *I Believe in the Holy Spirit*, to guide us in an initial exploration.

The Spirit of Yahweh was already present at creation, bringing order out of chaos. This same Spirit later formed Israel into a single people pledged to God in a covenant, of love. In the new covenant the Spirit overshadows Mary of Nazareth, and she conceives and brings forth her firstborn son.

When Jesus inaugurates his public mission, the Spirit is present as power and promise. The Spirit drives Jesus out into the desert and supports him in combat with Satan. The Spirit remains with Jesus throughout his ministry as he proclaims the kingdom in which all human beings, animated by that same Spirit, are to live in peace and harmony. The miracles of Jesus reveal the power of the Spirit not only to heal but to draw wounded people into the solidarity of community life.

The death and resurrection of Jesus occasions a new out-pouring of the Spirit which, as the Second Vatican Council said, "makes the Church grow, perpetually renews Her and leads Her to perfect union with Her spouse" (*Lumen Gentium*, #4). Guided by the Spirit, the Church remembers the solemn prayer of Jesus that "all may be one, Father, as you are in me and I am in you, so that the world may believe" (John 17:21). All baptized members of the Church, empowered by the Spirit, are coresponsible for forming the Church into a genuine community of worship and service. Thus the Church as the sacrament of the Spirit is called to be a visible sign of the unity of the whole human family and an instrument of reconciliation for all.

As this brief outline suggests, it is possible to reread the Scriptures with much greater emphasis on the role of the Holy Spirit. Some contemporary authors have also given greater prominence to the Spirit in their reflections on the Church. In this they are following Irenaeus, a second-century Church Father, who spoke of the Church as a sacrament of the Spirit.

Hans Küng has a section on the Church as the creation of the Spirit in his book *The Church*. He insists that freedom must be celebrated in the Church because it is God's gift to the community: "Where the Spirit of the Lord is, there is freedom" (2 Corinthians 3:17). This freedom must not lead to arbitrariness or license but to order and peace. Charisms are bestowed on individuals not for personal gain but for service. "To each is given the manifestation of the Spirit for the common good" (1 Corinthians 12:7).

The Brazilian liberation theologian, Leonardo Boff, has also developed the model of the Church as sacrament of the Spirit in his book *Church: Charisms and Power*. His emphasis is on the need for greater creativity and openness in the Church to counter the rigidity and formalism associated with the hierarchical institution. The charisms of all the members must be respected by the leaders and not extinguished. Clerical lead-

ers must not be allowed to co-opt all the gifts of the Spirit or
to use their power over the sacred rituals to control the people. Boff's provocative book offers fresh perspectives on the
problem of clericalism and suggests some exciting possibilities for faith communities which strive to be credible signs of
the Spirit.

In *Woman-Church* Rosemary Ruether points out that, from the
very beginning, the essential conflict within the Church has
been between the institutional model and the more charismatic approaches represented by the Corinthian model described in Paul's letters. A charismatic community strives to
be responsive to the promptings of the Spirit in all dimensions of its life. It treasures freedom and creativity while refusing to treat traditional structures as absolutes. When the
charismatic dimension is dominant, the community manifests
greater equality among its members and finds new energy
for spreading the kingdom.

In real life we don't have pure models; and seldom is the
battle between the good guys and the bad. Every parish is a
mixture of authority structures and charismatic gifts. The institutional Church with its hierarchy is not a separate entity
sharply divided from the community empowered by the
Spirit. Leadership is as much a charism as is prophecy. All
communities need some structure.

The real problem for parishes is to achieve a healthy balance
and a fruitful synthesis of institutional and charismatic elements. Judging by your letter, the authority/institutional dimension in your parish has simply overwhelmed the charismatic dimension.

This is not unusual and represents the general problem in the
Church today. We have a long way to go before we even approach a healthy balance between the institutional and the
Spirit-filled elements. Those of us who want to see this balance become a reality must find more effective ways to make
our case. We must show by word and example that the

whole Church benefits from enhancing the freedom and creativity associated with the Spirit.

At the practical level, however, this celebration of freedom and personal charisms remains a frightening prospect for many authority figures. The Spirit, which breathes where she will, cannot be controlled. In a parish striving to be a vibrant sacrament of the Spirit, the initiatives of individuals and groups are multiplied and intensified so that the official leaders cannot control them all, even if they try. This is a pragmatic solution to the messianic tendencies of authoritarian leaders!

Of course, abuses will occur in the Spirit model as they did in Corinth. This is inevitable. In a parish which fosters initiative and creativity, some people will misuse their freedom. With many diverse groups and activities, clear lines of communication are hard to maintain. Some programs will not fit neatly into a leadership flow chart. The whole operation will, at times, appear messy and disorganized—a lot like life itself. With a bow to Churchill, we could say that this model of Church is the worst type—except for its only alternative, which is a rigid structure devoid of life and energy.

In parishes where the balance is tipped more toward the charismatic dimension than the institutional, individuals must learn to live with a certain degree of ambiguity. An ability to tolerate mistakes and failures is also helpful. Leaders must be comfortable with individuals and groups taking initiative without asking for permission. Those in charge of particular areas of ministry must realize that they are not in charge of other areas—let alone the whole operation. A large vision and a sense of humor seem helpful when the communication inevitably breaks down and the messiness piles up. The Church as sacrament of the Spirit is not easily controlled or analyzed.

Rita, I realize that you are struggling with hurt and disappointment. You want practical advice—and I offer a new model of the Church! Still, perspective seems important when the wall appears so high and thick.

The Spirit, who empowers the Church, cannot finally be blocked or contained. Walls come tumbling down in strange ways and at odd times. Sometimes groups dedicated to consciousness-raising and structural change are able to make a difference. On other occasions, quiet conversions of the heart unleash surprising forces. If the Church really is the sacrament of the Spirit, then you are not alone in the struggle and the current situation in your parish cannot be the last word.

Chapter Two

Celebrating Unity-in-Diversity

---

1. Current Trends in Catholic Thought

Recently I had the opportunity tohear outstanding Catholic scholars including Richard McCormick, Avery Dulles, Richard McBrien, Lisa Cahill, Lawrence Cunningham, Anne Carr, Michael Novak, Arthur McGovern and Donald Senior, lecture on current trends in Catholic thought. These presentations provid excellent summaries on particular topics such as faith, Christ, church, scripture, morality, and spirituality. They also suggest some general characteristics or themes which invite further reflection.

Current Catholic thought continues to manifest its traditional preference for both-and approaches to theological questions, rather than the either-or often preferred by Protestant scholars. Catholicism at its best has a universal and inclusive character. It is a broad symbol system which encompasses competing tendencies. In opposition to the classic Protestant emphasis on scripture alone, faith alone, and grace alone, Catholic scholars continue to speak about both scripture and tradition, both faith and works, both grace and nature. This both-and mentality provides a framework for approaching other questions as well. The church is an institution and a charismatic community. We move toward the truth by faith and reason. Marriage is for the sake of parenthood and fostering mutual love. A healthy spiritual life has a contemplative and active component. One speaker, Fr. Richard McBrien, said he wanted "both-and" inscribed on his tombstone. Catholics faithful to their heritage have it inscribed in their minds as a framework for interpreting life.

Catholic thought is attuned to the sacramental character of reality. The infinite is found in the finite, the extraordinary in the ordinary. As the poet Gerard Manley Hopkins put it, ". . . the world is charged with the grandeur of God." Teilhard de Chardin expressed this Catholic sensibility by describing the material evolving universe as the "divine milieu" which manifests the radiance of God. The divine self-communication comes to us in and through created reality. The Gracious Mystery can be found in ordinary daily life. The Catholic imagination is fundamentally open to the signals of transcendence emanating from the sensible world. This general incarnational sense grounds the Catholic emphasis on the seven sacraments, and especially the Eucharist, as the focal point of piety and the springboard for action on behalf of the kingdom.

In Catholic thought today there is a growing recognition of pluralism. We are more aware of the pluralism that has always characterized Christian understanding. Mark's gospel, which emphasizes the hidden character of the suffering Messiah, sounds different to us than John's Gospel, which represents Jesus as the kingly Lord. The Eastern Fathers of the Church put more emphasis on the divinizing power of uncreated grace than did the Western Fathers. Bonaventure had a more mystical sense of the Christian life than did his 13th-century contemporary Thomas Aquinas, who presented the faith in a systematic and detached fashion. Today we can readily discern diverse schools and opinions within Catholic thought: remnants of classic Thomism; the liberationist perspectives of minorities and feminists; contemporary theological approaches best represented by Karl Rahner; post-modern probings which take seriously the electronic age and the environmental crisis; and theologies developed in the context of interreligious dialogue. We are familiar with diverse models of Christ and the Church. Believing persons of good will hold different opinions on questions of personal and social ethics. Some Catholics employ imaginative prayer forms while others use the mind-emptying methods of the East. An analysis of current trends in Catholic thought is necessarily complex because no single school of thought can totally dominate the discussion. The quest for wisdom is served when the diverse strains of thought are included in the conversation.

This evident pluralism has generated a new quest for unity within Catholicism which centers more on general sensibilities and characteristics than on specific doctrines or devotions. Thus we can identify a distinctive Catholic imagination which recognizes the sacramental character of the world, appreciates the value of tradition, has a positive view of human existence lived in community, treasures reason and philosophy in defending and promoting the faith, and accepts the value of the Pope as a focal point of unity. The search for unity also distinguishes dogmas from doctrines and general principles from concrete imperatives. It recognizes the hierarchy of truths in which, for example, the fundamental teachings on Christ are more important than the Marian doctrines. It is easier for Catholics to gather in unity around the most important truths of the faith stated in the broadest terms than around secondary doctrines formulated in the distinctive language of a particular theological school.

Current Catholic thought has a clear, personalistic tone. Faithful to the thrust of the teachings of Jesus, it has made persons more important than laws, structures, systems or institutions. Contemporary theology has made good use of the language and categories of modern existential thought. Human beings are interdependent, self-transcendent creatures who must freely and generously respond to the call of the living God. Jesus Christ is a truly human person who exemplifies the fullness of human maturity. Grace involves us in a relationship of intimacy with the triune God. Faith is personal dedication to Jesus Christ and his message. The church is a community of baptized persons who accept responsibility for making it a credible sign and instrument of the kingdom. Sacraments are encounters with the risen Lord. Christian morality proclaims the ideal of putting on the mind of Christ. Social justice insists that institutions and structures must serve the well-being of persons without leaving anyone out. In the life of heaven we find our final fulfillment as members of the family of God. This personalistic focus and language is designed to reflect the longings of our hearts and to engage us more fully in the quest for holiness.

Vatican II continues to function as a touchstone for Catholic thought and as a springboard for more creative approaches. From one perspective the Council summed up the great biblical, liturgical, theological and ecumenical movements of the 20th century. Catholic thinkers today frequently draw on particular aspects of this achievement, confident that the Council was a watershed event which legitimated the shift from classical to contemporary theology. But as Karl Rahner has taught us, the Council can also be seen as the tiny beginning of a great movement in which the Catholic community will become for the first time in its history a world church. We are on the threshold of an exciting new era in which Christianity will not be tied to its European and American forms but will be inculturated into diverse regions, nations and ethnic groups. The avant garde Catholic thinkers are taking this new perspective seriously. They are, for example, attempting to understand the precise role of Jesus within the universal salvific will of God, especially given our new appreciation of the significance of other prophets such as the Buddha and Mohammed. In other words, the Second Vatican Council is not simply the culmination of trends which are now well understood. It functions, rather, as the tentative beginning of a new creative period in Catholic theology.

The historical critical methods of reading the Bible developed by Scripture scholars during the last two centuries continue to play a vital role in Catholic thought. We understand Christ better today because we know more about the distinctive theologies of the four evangelists, Paul, and the other New Testament writers. The Church as a whole has greater freedom to carry out the task of reforming itself because New Testament scholarship has made clear that the early church organized itself in very diverse ways. While the historical method which emphasized the intent and societal setting of the biblical authors has proven valuable, more recent scholarship has emphasized that the biblical text has a life of its own and that readers today encounter it with their own distinctive concerns. The Gospels, for instance, can be read as wonderful, revelatory stories with a special message for poor people today, without knowing anything about the date or setting of their composition. Feminist scholars are using this approach to overcome the sexist bias found in the scriptures.

Catholic thought today reflects a growing recognition of the importance of symbol, story and ritual. Contemporary theologians accept the symbolic character of all religious language. To say that God is our Father does not mean that God is male or that patriarchy is justified. Leading scholars such as Bernard Cooke (cf. *The Distancing of God*) recognize that continuing liturgical reform is dependent on a better understanding of how ritual actually works. Influential authors have rediscovered Augustine's insight that personal stories can be used to communicate universal truths. Literal approaches to scriptures, creeds, and doctrines distort the meaning of religious truth and often lead to unnecessary conflicts. Symbolic interpretations remind us that all authentic religious statements point to a Mystery that remains inexhaustible and beyond human control. Catholic thought is at its best when it remembers that this Mystery is not only a sovereign master, but also a gracious presence guiding and sustaining the effort to humanize our world.

2. Diverse Mindsets: A Challenge for Dialogue

We all know the frustration of attempting serious conversation with another Christian, only to discover we are on totally different wavelengths. Why does this happen when we supposedly hold a common faith?

In the past these frustrations were usually attributed to denominational differences. Catholics and Protestants simply spoke a different language and viewed the world from different perspectives.

Today, however, these traditional denominational differences have blurred. Yet there are new sources of frustration. Liberal Catholics, for example, may now experience greater kinship with progressive Protestants than with conservative Catholics.

In trying to make sense out of this new situation, I continue to find a great deal of help in Bernard Lonergan's fundamental distinction between classical and contemporary mindsets. When two Catholics are arguing, for example, about the desirability of having grade-school children memorize the Ten Commandments, something deeper than educational technique is probably involved. If these two Catholics tried to clarify the basic presuppositions behind their positions on the Ten Commandments, two very different outlooks, or mindsets, would become evident.

Due to events in the modern world, such as industrialization, urbanization, secularization and the rise of science, there has been a revolution in fundamental outlook which some scholars call a "paradigm shift." This movement from a classical to a contemporary viewpoint involves various shifts: from the quest for certainty to a recognition of the value of approximation and probability; from understanding truth as timeless to seeing it as historically, culturally and personally conditioned; from a hierarchically-structured view of reality to an evolutionary outlook.

Christians with a classical mindset tend to live out and articulate their faith in a way quite different from those who have the more contemporary viewpoint. When disagreements arise—whether over large issues such as political involvement, economic policy and social justice or more intramural concerns such as liturgical reform and religious education approaches—it is often due to fundamentally divergent viewpoints.

Teilhard de Chardin gave us a helpful image for appreciating this modern shift in mindsets. Contemporary people, he said, are like those passengers below deck on a ship who are drawn up onto the top deck to discover, for the first time, that the whole ship is moving. The world, as well as the Christian message, looks much different from the evolutionary perspective provided by the top deck. Dialogue with those still below deck is difficult and demands both charity and attention to the great human issues which have a way of undercutting differences in viewpoint.

To understand the differences and disputes among Christians today, we have to know more about those above and those below deck. Lonergan's distinction between contemporary and classical mindsets provides an understanding of what distinguishes these individuals at the most fundamental level—and it invites further specification of precisely how a particular mindset translates into attitudes and behaviors.

Some of those below deck are becoming more vocal and aggressive. Their opposition to the contemporary mindset is well represented by those who insist that creationism be taught in the public schools along with the theory of evolution. Many have aligned themselves in a new partnership with the traditional American way of life. They speak uncritically of the value of capitalism, celebrate the work ethic and call for self-reliance. Their language often suggests that their approach is the only legitimate expression of Christian faith and that they are the only ones standing up for traditional values. This exclusive outlook certainly makes honest dialogue more difficult and threatens to poison the public debate.

Meanwhile, on the top deck, things are not as homogeneous as Teilhard's image might suggest. Christians who have made the shift to this new mindset tend to cluster in various groups based on common interests, perceptions of the evolutionary process, socioeconomic status and position in the Church. They are often bewildered by the new barriers that arise among people who share the common conviction that Christianity must respond constructively to the contemporary world. A clearer picture of these emerging groups is needed if we are to appreciate the differences and promote continued dialogue and cooperation on the top deck.

One top-deck cluster includes those we might call "ecumenical Christians." They tend to look for similarities in apparently diverse positions, for the commonness of the human situation, and for a God who is present in the whole of history. For them Christ is the ideal of human development as well as the divine Logos who continues to touch and gather all people.

Ecumenical Christians believe that the extraordinary is manifest in the ordinary and that the evil in the world is manageable. The universalist passages in the Bible, such as the prologue to John's Gospel, strike responsive chords in this group. Thomas Merton serves as a model for these ecumenical Christians, and the writings of Karl Rahner and Teilhard de Chardin express many of their deepest sentiments.

Members of this group must recognize, however, that they are subject to particular temptations. For example, they tend to gloss over real religious differences, to forget the transcendence of God, to fall into an excessively privatistic piety and to downplay the reality of evil in our world.

The top deck also include a group of "prophetic Christians." These believers are listening carefully for a call from the hidden and transcendent God who judges and saves a sinful world filled with contradictions. They feel the need for God's grace to heal human weakness and estrangement. For them Christ is the Savior who redeems us by his sufferings on the cross.

Prophetic Christians appreciate the biblical themes of judgment, the message of the prophets and the Pauline notion of justification by faith and not works. Daniel Berrigan is a contemporary figure who represents much of the substance and mood of this group. The great neo-orthodox theologians, such as Karl Barth and the Niebuhr brothers (Reinhold and H. Richard), provide a helpful theological expression of the sentiments of prophetic Christians.

The challenge for these Christians is to maintain hope in spite of their sense of evil and guilt. They must remain open to the current activity of the Spirit who unites all people and empowers us to help build the earth into a community of justice and love.

A third group which shares the contemporary outlook of the top deck are the "liberationist Christians." They begin with a keen awareness of the oppression and alienation produced by the modern world, especially through its unjust social structures. They view the present situation not as a crisis of faith but as a failure of *practice*. Only concrete action on behalf of the poor and oppressed can transform the modern situation. God is the Lord of the Exodus who continues to will social, political and economic liberation for all people.

Liberationist Christians see Christ as the liberator who comes to preach the Good News to the poor and to liberate the captives. They emphasize that the Spirit is at work in all the small Christian groups which apply the gospel to concrete social situations.

The martyred bishop Oscar Romero symbolizes the ideals of this group. Theologians such as Johann Metz, Gustavo Guttierez, Rosemary Radford Ruether, Leonardo Boff and James Cone articulate various aspects of biblical liberation from the perspective of the poor, the marginalized, minorities and women. Liberationist Christians have learned from experience the danger of falling into a mere humanism which ends up denying the sovereignty of God, the power of grace and the need for a rich spiritual and sacramental life.

Dialogue even among those Christians who share a contemporary mindset does not come easily. Top-deck conversation can be facilitated, however, by a better understanding of the presuppositions, interests, perspectives and languages of these various Christian groupings. It helps to remember that we are all dedicated to making the Christian message available and effective for our complex and fast-changing world.

Of course there are many ways to group and categorize the Christians on the top deck. All such models help direct our attention to general characteristics, tendencies, strengths and weaknesses. No individual fits perfectly into any of these types or categories. Successful dialogue always goes beyond such models to the uniqueness of the person.

3. Keeping Alive the Progressive Spirit of Vatican II

The times demand courage and perseverance from Catholics committed to the progressive reforms initiated by the Second Vatican Council. Those of us who knew the exhilaration of a new Pentecost when the Council closed in 1965 have a responsibility to keep alive that spirit of renewal for the younger generation. Individuals who have worked diligently to embody the dreams unleashed by the Council are now called to preserve and build on the conciliar vision.

The times are challenging for progressive Catholics. Polarization in our parishes continues to grow. Reactionaries, who are not interested in dialogue, resort to organized coercive measures to reverse the dominant spirit of the Council. Unfortunately, they exercise an influence which far exceeds both their numbers and the cogency of their arguments. Conservative Catholics claim that the tide is turning in their direction. They point to strong papal policies, new traditional bishops and firm Vatican reactions to dissent, as well as to the successes of conservative seminaries, religious orders and secular institutes, such as Opus Dei.

Historically, it is helpful to recall that Pope John XXIII called the Council, not as a defensive reaction against heresy, but as an opportunity to reform the Church, to open the windows for fresh air, to inaugurate a new Pentecost, to promote Christian unity and to adapt the formulation of the Christian message to the modern world. During the course of the Council, the bishops from around the world rejected the rigid, defensive documents prepared by the conservative curia. The debates in the Council generally showed that those favoring reform outnumbered the conservatives by a margin of about three to one.

When the bishops were unable to reach a consensus or a theological synthesis on disputed questions, they often adopted the strategy of simply including both progressive positions and traditional ones in the same document. On a number of occasions Pope Paul VI, who generally sided with the progressive majority, made concessions to the conservatives in order to secure their final approval of the documents. This helps explain why both progressives and conservatives can point to passages in the Council documents which support their divergent positions.

In the period after the Council, Pope John Paul VI found many ways to carry out and even enhance the progressive thrust of the Council. Thus he made important reforms in the curia, established an international theological commission, decreed that the vernacular could be used throughout the whole Mass, and wrote significant encyclicals on evangelization and social problems. From the liberal perspective, however, Pope Paul's encyclical on birth control, *Humanae Vitae*, proved to be a disaster. By going against the vast majority of the commission established to study this question, he dealt a severe blow to the progressive spirit engendered by the Council. After 1968, Mass attendance in the United States plummeted by twenty percentage points over the next seven years—a phenomenon which sociologist Andrew Greeley attributes to the promulgation of *Humanae Vitae*.

Despite their disappointment, many Catholics continued to work diligently for reform in the Church. Movements such as the charismatic renewal, Cursillo, Marriage Encounter and, later, RENEW, flourished, thus providing reform-minded Catholics with support and guidance.

With the election of Pope John Paul II in 1978, new challenges arose to the progressive spirit of the Council. The Pope seemed to be more influenced by his anti-Communist experience in Poland than by his participation in the Council. On the one hand, he has fashioned a truly radical social teaching which offers a striking critique of both collective systems such as Communism, which deny individual rights, and capitalistic systems, which breed individualism, materialism and consumerism. On the other hand, the Pope has moved in a more conservative direction on internal Church matters. His appointment of Cardinal Ratzinger as prefect of the Congregation for the Doctrine of the Faith in 1981 signaled a concentrated effort to centralize authority in the Vatican and to control reform movements throughout the Catholic world. In the United States this has produced a whole series of repressive measures which we associate with well-known names, such as Bishop Hunthausen, theologian Charles Curran and Archbishop Weakland. Vatican opposition to optional celibacy, the ordination of women and the new pastoral approaches to the Sacrament of Penance continue to hurt the morale of progressive Catholics.

In response to these distressing trends, reform-minded Catholics are called to work courageously and resolutely to sustain and revitalize the progressive spirit of Vatican II. The Council remains for us a great source of guidance and inspiration. The *Dogmatic Constitution on the Church* teaches us that the Church is a sacrament of the kingdom and that it must always be reforming itself. We are all the People of God, equal members of the Church through our Baptism, participants in the one priesthood of Christ. Infallibility rests in the *whole* Church: "the body of the faithful as a whole, anointed as they are by the Holy One cannot err in matters of faith" (No. 12).

By emphasizing the collegial relationship between the Pope and the bishops, the Council gives us a sense of the importance and the power of collaborative approaches at all levels of Church life. When the bishops very consciously taught that the one Church of Christ "subsists in the Catholic Church" (No. 8), they implicitly recognized the ecclesial status of other Christian bodies, thereby opening up the possibility for greater ecumenical dialogue and cooperation.

The *Dogmatic Constitution on Divine Revelation* ratified the thrust of modern biblical interpretation and encouraged us to study the Scriptures. By insisting that the human person has a right to religious freedom and cannot be coerced by any human power, the *Declaration on Religious Freedom* validated our American experience of religious liberty and brought this notion into the consciousness of the whole Church. The *Constitution on the Sacred Liturgy*, which opened up the possibility of ongoing liturgical reform, reminds us of the centrality of the Eucharist in Catholic life and makes participation in the sacraments the key to reform. In the *Declaration on the Relationship of the Church to Non-Christian Religions*, the Council fathers taught us to be open to the truth and goodness found in all the world's great religious traditions. Finally, the great *Pastoral Constitution on the Church in the Modern World* reminds us that believers must be passionately involved in the task of transforming the world, and that we will find our holiness in the struggle for justice and peace.

A whole program of progressive renewal in the Church is sketched out by the Council documents. There is no doubt that the dominant thrust of the Council was in the direction of reform.

Progressives understand that this reform is ongoing, that the task of adapting our presentation of the Christian message to changing conditions in the world is a continuing one. Reform is not something accomplished once and for all so that we have a neat tidy package to hand on to the next generation. Christianity is a dynamic force which must serve as a leaven in every new age and culture. We best serve the next generation by sharing with them the dynamic spirit of the gospel unleashed by the Council, not by a slavish repetition of conciliar texts.

In one of his most influential essays, the great German Jesuit Karl Rahner insisted that the Second Vatican Council was not merely the culmination of previous movements, but rather the *initial stage* of a grand movement in which the Church would become, for the first time in its history, a truly World Church, a community of faith incarnated in all cultures. From this perspective, the conservative project of centralizing authority in the Vatican and spreading a uniform interpretation of the faith throughout the world appears totally anachronistic.

Rahner's theological interpretation of the Council suggests that the progressive spirit will eventually triumph. We find intimations supporting this conviction in diverse signals of hope scattered throughout the Catholic world: committed lay ministers, vibrant progressive parishes, prayerful contemporary liturgies, open ecumenical dialogues, inspiring prayer groups, fruitful Scripture discussions and dedicated action on behalf of peace and justice.

The current struggle demands that reform-minded Catholics stand up to the reactionaries who employ scare tactics. We must do so with a resolute courage, which remains charitable and open to the possibility of civil discourse. We must try to turn polarization into constructive dialogue. It is important to see Catholic conservatives as partners in the task of building up the Body of Christ and spreading the cause of God in the world.

Our conservative friends enrich the progressive project by reminding us of the importance of tradition, by helping us recognize ambiguities in the culture and by forcing us to refine our own efforts to adapt our proclamation of the Christian message in the modern world. In the project of reforming the Church, we must support one another as we strive to remain faithful to the Lord.

Prayer and reflection help to keep our priorities straight and our hopes high. The current challenges can, indeed, weigh us down: but they also provide the opportunity for courageous witness based on trust in the renewing power of the God who accomplishes new and surprising things.

4. The Quest for Religious Solidarity: Dialogue With a Convert

Changes in the Church have created special problems for some converts to Catholicism, as the following dialogue indicates.

Theologian: Our world is increasingly pluralistic and therefore Christian people must learn to tolerate—even celebrate—a diversity of worldviews, theologies, philosophies, life-styles and spiritualities.

Convert: But where is the glue? In such a pluralistic situation, what holds the Christian community together? What symbols are held in common? What factors shape a common understanding and give a sense of belonging to a distinct group? How do we know if we really hold similar values and how do we express and manifest them if we do?

When I joined the Catholic community many years ago, one of the things that attracted me was its solidity, its homogeneous character, its claim to be an all-embracing way of life. It seemed like a neat and tidy package that could provide a solid basis for dealing with the rest of my confusing world. Now, much of that has been taken from me. I feel uprooted, adrift and even angry at people like you who seem to be tearing my world apart.

Theologian: I know you feel strongly about this, and I am glad we can still talk despite the anger. But I see no solution in a nostalgic return to the past. Your need for roots cannot be satisfied by imposing a new legal and liturgical uniformity (whether progressive or conservative) on the Catholic Church. We have to find "the glue" by refocusing on the core message of Christianity. Our task is to establish solidarity by reappropriating the central symbols and by renewing our traditional rituals.

I agree with you that a religion is an integrated symbol system which should provide people with a sense of community, a shared value system and a common interpretation of life. Religious symbols, stories and rituals do give us a sense of solidarity and a framework for making sense out of our experience. As the great Lutheran theologian Paul Tillich insisted, religion indeed functions as the substance of culture. And when religion loses its power, the culture tends to disintegrate.

Convert: That's precisely what makes me wonder if the bishops at the Second Vatican Council really knew what they were doing. The neo-conservative author Michael Novak once called the Council "a disaster." He said it did what wars and heresies couldn't do: destroy "the very meaning of Catholicism as a coherent people with a coherent vision." It seems to me that the Council has helped to loosen the glue which held the Church and society together.

Theologian: I think that judgment is misguided. The Council needs to be seen, in historical perspective, as the tentative and flawed beginning of the Church's effort to come to terms with our pluralistic and evolving world.

Surely mistakes were made by the bishops and by their theological interpreters. Perhaps, in their dialogue with existential philosophy and humanistic psychology, they paid too little attention to the insights of the sociologists who remind us of the conserving and integrating role of religious symbols and stories. But the effort to enter into dialogue with the contemporary world was, in my opinion, necessary, and the conversation must continue.

To our benefit, the renewal fostered by the Council has highlighted the core of the Christian message: that the Mystery surrounding us is gracious and has spoken to us through Jesus of Nazareth, the risen Lord, whose continuing presence to all people is proclaimed by the Church. A healthy reordering of priorities has also taken place. Thus Jesus Christ takes precedence over the saints, the Eucharist over private devotions, and the law of love over Church laws.

We now have a great opportunity to gather around these fundamental teachings, to achieve a sense of solidarity informed by the essential symbols and to join in common action on behalf of justice and peace. And, as important theologians insist, our fundamental Christian symbols, stories and rituals still have the power to bind us together and to form us into a people with an illuminating and inspiring worldview.

Convert: But what does this approach do to the distinction between Catholics and Protestants? I joined the Church because it seemed different—more liturgically oriented, a richer devotional life, more definite teaching, a stronger authority structure. Now those things seem to be disappearing.

Theologian: Most of the historical disputes are losing their power to divide Protestants and Catholics. But I see this as part of a constructive movement toward the kind of Christian unity which Jesus desired for his followers. Besides, if we want Christianity to be a positive force in the culture and part of the glue which holds society together, then we need to achieve as much unity as possible. It is important to speak with a single voice so that we present a united front against anti-gospel tendencies.

I understand your desire to be part of a distinctive people; this inclination is no doubt shared by many Christians. Perhaps we could respond to this natural human desire by moving toward a unified Church in which traditional groupings maintain their distinctive pieties and practices while agreeing on the essential teachings. We Catholics, for example, would contribute to the overall richness of the united Church by maintaining our sacramental sense of life and worship, while Presbyterians, for instance, would maintain their great emphasis on the scriptural Word. And when confronted with a common problem, such as the growing homelessness in our country, all Christian groups would gather together to respond cooperatively in justice and charity to such tragic human suffering.

Convert: But the real problem is that so many Christians don't feel personally supported or motivated by the core teachings and symbols. I myself feel estranged, as though I were roaming around in unfamiliar territory.

Theologian: Christian symbols do not float free; they are encountered, ingested and manifested in a local congregation. They must be appropriated within particular faith communities. We celebrate the Lordship of Jesus, the normative character of the Scriptures and the centrality of the Eucharist with a specific group of people in a particular place with a distinctive tone or atmosphere.

If the general atmosphere of a parish is warm and inviting, then the symbols have a better chance of capturing people's imaginations and linking them together in common values and activities. My guess is that if you felt more at home in your parish, were more involved, and were getting more positive messages there, you would feel less alienation. I know many people who find their parish to be a source of strength and rootedness as well as a catalyst for growth and development. They have found a bit of the glue you are looking for.

Convert: That sounds nice but my parish is so big and impersonal that I do not even know most of the people. I often feel isolated and alone attending Mass with hundreds of other people. There is not much sense of solidarity in that.

Theologian: I am sure many people can identify with that description. It reminds me of the value of smaller communities. Many persons I know who do feel a genuine sense of religious solidarity find it through small group activities such as serving on a significant parish committee, working with others on a common service project, participating regularly in a prayer group, or sharing a group experience weekend such as Cursillo or Christ Renews His Parish. In such settings the core of Christianity takes on a deeper communal meaning and power. The story of Jesus retold in a vibrant parish setting becomes a source of solidarity. The Eucharist celebrated at the end of a day of service to the poor is clearly a communal meal. The familiar scriptural passage read during a weekend encounter becomes a shared bit of good news. In all these situations, the traditional symbols demonstrate their power to create community by invoking a sense of solidarity, providing roots and offering a shared vision.

These activities are most effective when they include opportunities for personal exchanges which move beyond the superficial to reveal the true depth of ordinary experience. When we encounter one another at these deeper levels, we come to know the remarkable power of the unifying Spirit who is the deepest source of all human bonding.

Although this small-group approach runs the risk of creating elite enclaves within a parish, it does offer more realistic possibilities for experiencing community than a nostalgic return to the supposed uniform Catholic world of the past. Our best chance of finding the glue you seek is in a renewed sense of solidarity based on common experiences, sustained and illuminated by the essential Christian symbols.

5. A Catholic Without Embarrassment

Working out a contemporary spirituality for a pluralistic world means addressing questions about how to relate the particular to the universal. How can I be rooted in the Christian faith and, at the same time, be open to other religious traditions and worldviews? How can I be a genuine Catholic and enter into honest dialogue with my Protestant, Jewish and Muslim friends? If a religion makes comprehensive claims to possess God's truth, how can its adherents expect to learn anything from another tradition?

John Murray Cuddihy offered an interesting approach to this problem in his book *No Offense: Civil Religion and Protestant Taste.* His ideas can help us come to a better understanding of our position as Catholics living in a pluralistic society.

Cuddihy begins with an analysis of this oft-repeated phrase: "I just happen to be Catholic." Why do Catholics in the United States use this kind of language which seems to reflect a fear or reticence about admitting particular religious differences? Cuddihy thinks there is a pervasive "religion of civility" in our country which implicitly forbids the celebration of particularity—especially any notion of exclusivity or superiority.

Cuddihy takes the civil religion theme—originated by Rousseau and popularized in the United States by Robert

Bellah (*Beyond Belief*)—and gives it a new twist. Instead of focusing on a distinct civil religion with its sacred texts (Constitution), saints (Jefferson) and holydays (Thanksgiving), Cuddihy discerns a pervasive Protestant-inspired "religion of civility" which moderates all ostentation and insists that no one give offense in the public arena.

Although this religion of civility is sometimes viewed positively by the cultured elite as a desirable form of sophisticated charity, it generally functions negatively as a muted religion of polite manners, superficial community and bland morality. Cuddihy thinks this powerful and comprehensive religion of civility flows from distinctively Protestant attitudes and is tacitly imposed on Catholics and Jews in the United States. Whatever the true source of this unwritten code of civility, however, it does produce embarrassment over religious particularities.

So what particular embarrassments does the phrase "I just happen to be a Catholic" conceal? Here are just a few possibilities: the U.S. bishops speaking out on economic issues; the Vatican statement on homosexuality; traditional teaching on Mary, the saints, confession and purgatory; pacifist priests; curia treatment of dissident theologians; devotions such as the rosary, novenas and stations; authoritarian pastors; the papal teaching on birth control; ostentatious liturgical ceremonies; arm-waving charismatics; the wealth of the Church; Catholics who promote natural family planning; bingo; the pro-life movement; nuns in habits; historical events such as the Inquisition and the Crusades.

This brief listing suggests that the task of accepting Catholic particularity is an immense one. We have a long and checkered history as well as a rich and expanding diversity. We must face our own past in order to live authentically and openly today.

Cuddihy suggests another negative effect of the religion of civility: It forces a split personality—a bland, common-denominator *public* posture alongside a *private* existence where religious particularities are real. Questions like the following provide material for an enlightening phenomenology of religious embarrassment: Are there aspects of our actual belief system which we hide in public? Are there topics that can't be discussed at work or in social gatherings? Do we sense any unhealthy discrepancies between our public and private selves? Do we as Catholics feel pressure to conform to some unwritten cultural norms in order to be acceptable? Have we come to terms with an immigrant experience which encountered the so-called "nativist prejudice"?

In this context Cuddihy examines three American religious thinkers—the great Protestant theologian Reinhold Niebuhr, the influential Catholic theologian Father John Courtney Murray, and the important Jewish thinker Rabbi Arthur Hertzberg. Cuddihy tries to show how each sold out (that is, accommodated his theology) to the religion of civility.

Niebuhr, Cuddihy claims, sold out by renouncing the traditional Christian intention to convert the Jews. Murray made his accommodation by abandoning the traditional Catholic position on Church-State relations (which expected special privilege for the Church) and by reinterpreting the teaching that there is no salvation outside the Church. Hertzberg bowed to the religion of civility by playing down the Jewish claim to be the chosen people. Cuddihy charges that these men thus gave up essential elements in their religious traditions in order to be able to live comfortably in the United States.

Cuddihy assumes here that both Christianity and Judaism have exclusive claims that rule out genuine tolerance and honest dialogue. To affirm these claims is to be offensive; to deny them is to be dishonest.

Take, for example, the Catholic doctrine that "outside the Church there is no salvation." Cuddihy contends that since this is an obviously offensive claim in the pluralistic United States, Catholics, rather than being true to this doctrine, have sold out by muting their exclusive claims. Cuddihy's contention is reflected in the charges of other critics that American Catholics have made too many concessions to the dominant culture.

The problem with Cuddihy's position is that it is based on an outmoded theology. It falsely presumes that both Judaism and Christianity necessarily claim a monopoly on God's truth and an exclusive revelation which makes all other religions false and a pluralistic coexistence dishonest.

A more adequate theology is available which challenges both Cuddihy's assumptions and his conclusions. This theology understands that God wills the salvation of *all* people and freely gives the Spirit to every human being for this purpose. This divine presence in the human heart modifies the individuals' consciousness and produces an inner word which enlightens, inspires and calls for a response. When a person honestly answers this call of conscience, it is true to say that faith is present and that a step toward salvation has been taken. When this faith is accurately articulated, the truth is brought to light. When a community forms around this truth, it becomes a legitimate vehicle for both divine revelation and salvation.

From this theological perspective, no community can claim that it totally comprehends the divine truth nor that it has articulated it in the best possible way. There is a universal revelation present in our world, but it is always grasped in a limited and partial way. Particular communities will claim to have a fuller, or purer, or more comprehensive hold on God's truth; but this does not vitiate the point already established that an exclusive monopoly on divine truth is impossible.

Honest dialogue is therefore possible with other religious traditions precisely because they also possess valid insights into the divine human relationship—insights perhaps forgotten or overlooked by others. From this perspective, Niebuhr, Murray and Hertzberg do not appear as traitors to their religious heritage but as pioneers trying to work out the implications of a legitimate theology.

Fortunately we do not have to choose between living the exclusive particularism of the religious ghetto and the bland universalism of the American melting pot. It is possible for Catholics to be so deeply rooted in their religious tradition that they are thereby able to perceive truth, goodness and beauty wherever it is to be found. We can achieve a healthy universalism which appreciates that divine truth is always historically, culturally and personally conditioned.

There is a way to be proudly Catholic without being arrogant, to be open-minded without being mindless, to be a full participant in American life without claiming privilege, to be true to one's heritage without being exclusive. We can be genuinely Catholic without neurotic embarrassment.

6. Learning from the Curran Case: Theological and Cultural Factors

Now that the disputes surrounding Fr. Charles Curran have faded from the public consciousness, we might profit from a sober analysis of why individuals adopted such dramatically opposed views on the controversial questions involved in the case. Such an examination should also help us understand other conflicts between the Vatican and progressive Catholics in the United States.

1. The polarized opinions on the Curran case no doubt are related to different understandings of the fundamental nature of the Church. The familiar distinction between the institutional and communal models of the Church can guide our analysis. Those whose consciousness is shaped by the institutional model tend to value centralized power and clear lines of authority. They look for a clear, definite, unified message from the Pope and the bishops, based on the conviction that this is the most effective way of proclaiming the Gospel. Their dominant sense is of a universal Church, anchored in papal authority, which spreads throughout the world from its base in Rome. In this hierarchical model, there is more emphasis on the authority of the Roman curia and the local bishop than on international synods and national bishops' conferences. Individuals who espouse this ecclesiastical model were predisposed to side with Cardinal Ratzinger and to view Curran as a dissident who was undercutting the clear authority of the Church.

On the other hand, those of us who supported Curran tended to operate out of a different understanding of the Church. We speak easily of the Church as a faith community in which all the baptized are equal members with distinctive charisms for building up the Body of Christ. In proclaiming the Gospel, we are very mindful of the need to listen to the signs of the times and to adapt the gospel to the situation of people living today in our culture. The local Church is important in our thinking because it is a genuine realization of the Body of Christ in a given place. We can see certain values in the Eastern approach which begins with autonomous local churches joined together to form the one universal Church. Since we are looking for more democratic procedures in the Church, we support the development of a strong national bishops' conference. Pluralism, in our estimation, is not a threat to unity but the proper way to avoid a stifling uniformity, while creating a healthy diversity-in-unity. With this communal model of the Church structuring our outlook, we naturally tend to access Curran's position favorably. Even if we did not agree with all of his particular opinions, we thought he should be free to continue his work at Catholic University especially since his theology espoused respect for authority with honest inquiry. His insistence that the ethical demands of the Gospel function as ideals rather than strict laws provides us with helpful guidance in living out the Catholic faith in the real world. His willingness to deal with complex cases and possible exceptions offers comfort to ordinary people facing exceptional demands. For us, the Curran case highlights both the threat to Gospel values posed by authoritarianism in the Church, and the need to work for a Church which respects pluralism and individual charisms.

2. Our differences on the Curran case are also connected with the way we relate to our distinctive experience as citizens of the United States. In my experience, those who uphold the Vatican position are the same ones who generally tend to celebrate the power and strength of the United States. Our role in the past as a light to the nations and a defender against communism seemed natural and fitting to

them. They believe our presidents are right on target when they manifest strength and firmness against our adversaries, just as Pope John Paul and the Roman Curia are on target by dealing firmly with American dissidents like Curran. The relationship between these societal and ecclesiastical attitudes is obviously complex and there are surely individuals who do not fit the consistent profile. My own sense is that those who do are working out of what Bernard Lonergan called a "classical mindset," which generally views the world in static terms, thinks of truth as timeless and treasures certitude and order. In other words, classicists are consistent in looking for strong, authoritative statements from leaders in both society and church.

By way of contrast, those of us who supported Curran are clearly influenced by the positive experience of freedom and pluralism in the United States. In defending Curran, we tended to recall the example of John Courtney Murray, S.J., who, although silenced by the Vatican, still succeeded in bringing our distinctive understanding of religious liberty into the official consciousness of the whole Church. Along this same line, we hope to see Church structures reflect more of the democratic procedures which have served us well in this country. Our emphasis is not so much on the power of the United States but rather on the unity and diversity which we as a nation have achieved. We think the Church can learn lessons from our national experiment with maximizing freedom and celebrating diversity. Our imaginations are shaped by images of pluralism in action. We might recall for example, the pictures of Ronald Reagan and Jimmy Carter, bitter foes on many issues, trading compliments and good-natured barbs during their joint appearance at the Carter Library. This type of experience often repeated in the political arena predisposes us to look for unity in essential ends while vigorously debating the means to achieve these goals. Those of us who supported Curran instinctively wondered why this approach cannot be more operative in the Church. Dismissing him from his teaching post seemed to us to be narrow, rigid and short-sighted. We believe progress is made on difficult moral questions through continuing dialogue among theological peers and not by Vatican decree. This position is no doubt rooted in Lonergan's "contemporary mindset" which views the world in dynamic terms, while recognizing that truth is historically, culturally and personally conditioned. From this perspective, it is fitting to allow our experiences as citizens of a pluralistic democracy to influence the way we perceive our higher allegiance as members of the Catholic Church.

The Curran case is part of the larger history of the relationship between the Vatican and progressive elements in the Catholic Church in the United States. As we continue to wrestle with these kinds of questions, it will be helpful to uncover the philosophical, theological, and cultural assumptions which shape our own position on individual issues.

7. Characteristics of Catholicism

While the majority of Catholics are generally pleased with the reforms introduced by the Second Vatican Council, some still find themselves confused by the new openness and pluralism. Before the Council, Catholics inhabited a clear, precisely-defined world of Latin Masses, Friday abstinence, strict morality, Marian devotions, habited nuns, celibate clergy, regular Confession and uniform beliefs. Catholic identity was well established, providing individuals with a sense of belonging and a fixed frame of reference.

By way of contrast, Catholics today inhabit a loose, fluid pluralistic world. Many of the distinctive identifying characteristics have not only been abandoned in practice, but have also faded from consciousness. Few are missed in themselves. The cumulative effect, however, is striking. For some, the new situation is exciting and liberating, while for others it brings doubt and confusion. For all, it presents a new challenge to work out a viable Catholic identity in the contemporary world.

Being Catholic is a way of being human, religious, theistic and Christian. Thus, for example, we hold common cause with those humanists who respect the dignity and worth of individual persons, insisting that this fundamental respect be extended to human beings at all stages of the life cycle. With other religiously-oriented persons, we sense that there are mysterious depths in human existence which exceed rational calculation and are best handled through myth, symbol and ritual. With Jews, Moslems and other Christians, we believe in the one God who created the world and who will bring the process of history to a successful conclusion. This God, ultimately mysterious, is trustworthy and can be addressed in prayer. With our Orthodox and Protestant friends, we believe that this loving and merciful God has spoken most clearly in Jesus of Nazareth, the final prophet and absolute savior. We dedicate ourselves to Christ and his teachings, trying to live out his love in the world. In the faith community, we gather to hear the Word and to commemorate the Lord's Supper.

In addition to these common beliefs, it is helpful to explore other traits of the Catholic people (cf. *Catholicism* by Richard McBrien). Perhaps a general profile will emerge which will strike responsive chords with Catholics of diverse outlooks and pieties.

1. We Catholics have a sense that the Christian community needs a spokesperson who can enunciate Gospel ideals, as well as a focal point of unity which can hold the Church together. The Bishop of Rome performs that function for us, continuing the role of Peter in the New Testament period. Catholics disagree on exactly how this ministry should be exercised. Some want strong leadership, while others fear centralization and authoritarianism. Still, recognizing the dangers of fragmentation, we generally appreciate the value of a unified hierarchical structure in the Church which includes the papal office.

2. The Catholic community, historically, has emphasized the length and breadth of the Christian tradition. We tap the riches and carry the burden of a graced but sinful Church with a 2000-year history. The achievements of Augustine and Aquinas, as well as the sinfulness of the Crusades and Inquisition, are components in our collective memory. For us,

the tradition embodied in the ongoing life of the community is an important criterion for interpreting the Scriptures which remain normative for Christian life. In the Catholic community, the richness of the devotional tradition is preserved, ranging from the mysticism of John of the Cross and Teresa of Avila to the Marian piety derived from Lourdes and Fatima. Catholics pray the Office and the rosary, receive ashes and palms, and ask blessings for pregnant women and Easter food. At our best, we understand that tradition is a great storehouse from which we can freely select resources to enrich our Christian life today.

3. Catholics expect to experience God in and through the material world. Divine grace is mediated to us through visible signs. God deals with us as social, bodily creatures who encounter the infinite through the finite. Thus Catholicism is a heavily sacramental religion. The sacraments structure the development of Catholic life from Baptism through First Communion, Confirmation and Marriage to the Anointing of the Sick. While Catholicism knows its own brand of individualism, the sacramental system creates a communal sense of Christianity in which it is clear that God saves us as a member of a people. The Eucharist, frequently celebrated, is the gathering point and the sustaining energy for Catholic life. For us, Christ's manifold and real presence in the Eucharist is a sign of the triumphant power of God's love in the world. While Scripture and preaching have fortunately been given a renewed emphasis in the Catholic community, the primary proclamation of the Word is linked with the sacred meal as an essential element in the one act of sacramental worship. When Catholics celebrate the most significant events of their lives, they instinctively turn to the Eucharist as the way of expressing joy and commitment, as well as of managing grief and sorrow. In short, our religion is sacramental because we are convinced that God is incarnate in the world, sanctifying and transforming our bodily material existence.

4. At its best, the Catholic tradition has a healthy, positive sense of human nature, which grows out of this same incarnational principle that God is intimately present to his

creation. The Baptist theologian, Langdon Gilkey, describes the Catholic love of life, appreciation of the body, and ability to celebrate joyfully (cf. *Catholicism Confronts Modernity*). Irish wakes and Polish weddings come to mind, as does Belloc's line, "Wherever the Catholic sun does shine, there will be merriment and good wine." In an age struggling with chemical dependency and compulsive behavior, glib talk about this characteristic should obviously be avoided. Nevertheless, our theology clearly promotes a positive view of creation by emphasizing that grace divinizes human nature, transforms our world, and triumphs over all sin. The viewpoint is exemplified in the Catholic celebration of the power of reason and philosophy to defend and elucidate the faith. Far from being an obstacle to belief, our God-given intelligence can enable us to penetrate more deeply the mystery of the divine-human relationship. Augustine's use of Platonism, Aquinas' assimilation of Aristotle, and Karl Rahner's employment of existential thought remind us of the potential value of reason and philosophy for enhancing our faith. An honest examination of this Catholic characteristic must note that this prevailing sense of the goodness of God's creation has often broken down in the area of human sexuality. Negative attitudes flowing from Augustine's pessimistic outlook on sexuality have often overwhelmed the more consistent position that all aspects of human nature possess a fundamental goodness. Fortunately, we have in our tradition resources for developing healthier attitudes toward human sexuality.

5. Finally, Catholicism understands itself as a universal religion, able to be embodied in diverse cultures and open to truth, goodness, and beauty wherever they are to be found. This note of universality has, at times, been undercut by Roman insistence on uniformity. Today, however, it is clear that Catholicism is, indeed, a world-Church, with a role in world history and with the capacity to incorporate diverse national mentalities and indigenous expressions of the Christian faith into its common life. In other words, Catholicism is not confined to Europe and America, but can find a home and be a force for good in Africa, Asia and other parts of

the world as well. Furthermore, universality suggests that the Catholic Church is not a sect withdrawn from the world, but a community actively engaged in trying to transform and reconcile all segments of the human family and all aspects of human existence. This fundamental outlook on the Church's relationship to the world has spawned the great social teachings of the Catholic hierarchy during the past century.

In a complex and changing world, we Catholics must root our common identity in fundamental truths and practices and not in accidental and transient matters. We are a people unified in our commitment to Jesus Christ, sensitized to the presence of God in our world, and convinced of the potential value of a structured community which nourishes our faith, worship and service.

8. Selective Catholics: Taking Their Experience Seriously

Frank does not like the name "cafeteria Catholic," but he has to admit that this descriptive phrase fits his current outlook in the faith he received from his parents. There is no doubt he is Catholic. He has no intention of ever leaving the Church. He cannot imagine himself as a Lutheran or a Methodist or even an Episcopalian. When he is in the hospital, he wants to be visited by a Catholic priest and to receive Communion. Catholicism is in his bones and blood. His imagination is shaped by First Communions and Confirmations, by Catholic weddings and funerals and by the countless weekend Masses he has attended. Although he sometimes jokes about the repression he experienced during his 12 years in Catholic schools, he knows that they helped form his religious outlook on life. Frank thinks of his parish as his spiritual home and goes to Mass there regularly.

On the other hand, there is a "cafeteria" aspect to his connection with the Church. He simply cannot accept everything the Pope and the bishops have to say. For him, the problem began over 20 years ago when the Pope issued the birth control encyclical. He did not agree with the total ban on contraception then, and he does not accept it now. At first, the Pope's strict teaching, which seemed to discount his own experience as a married man, hurt him deeply and caused intense anger. All of that is past now. He is no longer angry at the Pope or bishops. When they say something on divorce or homosexuality or test-tube babies which contradicts his own experience or considered judgment, he simply tunes them out. In his mind, the official leaders in the Catholic Church no longer stand on pedestals nor are they infallible guides for his life. Given his liberal tendencies, he was especially happy with the pastoral letters of the American bishops on peace and the economy. Some of the papal statements on social policies and international relationships have also made sense to him.

By way of contrast, he almost automatically dismisses anything the Pope and bishops have to say about sex, love and marriage. There is no doubt that he does pick and choose among the various teachings of the Church. Moreover, he now goes to confession very infrequently and even misses Mass on occasion without feeling any guilt at all. A few years ago, he wondered if this whole approach was legitimate and authentic, but now he simply accepts it as a fact of modern Catholic life. Finally, he resents anyone who tries to tell him that he is not a good Catholic or that he should leave the Church. For him, the Church is like a family which should continue to make room for him.

Frank is typical of a large number of American Catholics who disagree with some Church teachings, but continue to call themselves Catholics. For example, of the 52 million registered Catholics, 66% disagree with the official opposition to the use of contraceptives, 64% think the Church should liberalize its position on divorce and 59% think that the priesthood should be open to married men (cf. *The Emerging Parish* by Joseph Gremillion and Jim Castelli). If we factor in the selective rejection of official Catholic social teaching by conservative Catholics, we get an even better sense of the extent of the disagreement with the Church.

Despite this widespread dissent from official positions, about 80% of the 67 million American who identify themselves as Catholics are registered in parishes. The rate of departures from the Catholic Church has remained almost constant for the last 30 years. Only one out of seven people born Catholic is no longer a member of the Church and about half of these have left because of mixed marriages. Furthermore, only about 6% of those who are still in the Church indicate that they might leave and most of these are thinking of leaving not because of the controversial issues such as birth control, but because of a perceived lack of spiritual and moral leadership.

These statistics do not reveal emotional responses or indicate how many people have made the easy accommodation with the institutional Church described by Frank. No doubt, some of the dissenters are angry and frustrated and others feel pangs of guilt. However, many analysts think there are a growing number of Catholics who simply follow their own conscience while maintaining a very loose relationship to the official Church leadership. They draw selectively on the resources found in the Catholic tradition without feeling constrained by doctrines and disciplines which do not accord with their experience. The Mass is a source of meaning and energy to them, but they do not feel bound by the Sunday obligation. In short, large numbers of dissenters continue to think of themselves as Catholics and find no compelling reason to leave the Church.

Let us examine in greater detail this widespread and significant development in the contemporary Church. We can begin by trying to name it properly. The term "cafeteria Catholic" is misleading and offensive, and therefore should be abandoned. Sociologist Andrew Greeley, who first identified and described this particular subgroup within the Church, spoke initially of "communal Catholics," emphasizing their identification with the Church as a community rather than as an institution. Later, he turned to the designation "selective Catholics," which suggests the free decision made by these believers about their faith. Both of these terms seem preferable to the abstract phrase "Culture Two Catholics," recently introduced by psychologist Eugene Kennedy (cf. *Tomorrow's Catholics, Yesterday's Church*) as a label for Catholics who find the Church as an institution largely irrelevant, but accept the Church as a sacramental source of meaning and inspiration.

The phrase "selective Catholic" reminds us that all believers deal selectively with their religious tradition at the personal and existential level. No Catholic personally appropriates every doctrine and practice of the faith. Some elements of our religion simply never penetrate our consciousness or influence our daily behavior. Even a bishop may find, for example. that the credal statement "he descended into hell" has never entered his prayer life or shaped his pastoral practice. We all meditate on particular favorite images of Christ, while neglecting other, equally valid images. Certain devotions appeal to us, while others leave us cold. Both consciously and unconsciously we select out certain doctrines and practices which enlighten and inspire us, while ignoring or neglecting other important aspects of our rich and diverse religious heritage. In this situation it is important to stay open to the potential value of the unappropriated doctrines and practices, recognizing that no matter how receptive we are, some elements of the tradition will always remain unassimilated. From this perspective, the gap definitely narrows between selective Catholics and those who identify more closely with the institution. None of us possesses the whole of the Catholic heritage, and all of us should stay open to the entire tradition.

In his story of Culture Two Catholics, Kennedy insists they are not rebellious people, but rather are looking to their Catholic tradition for spiritual guidance and nourishment. Having distanced themselves psychologically from the institution, they still believe that the Catholic heritage has important resources which can help them make sense out of their ordinary experience and can guide their everyday decisions. Although they do not give much attention to the latest statements of the Vatican or to ecclesiastical politics, they do treasure the sacramental life of the Church. The Eucharist which continues to shape their imaginations remains central to their spiritual life. The faith which is celebrated at Mass gives them a sense of identity. The gathering for the parish liturgy helps to satisfy their needs for association and community. These Catholics have learned to wait out poor homilies, but are delighted when the preaching illumines their experience and provides practical guidance for living as a Christian in the world. They want the liturgical life in their parishes to reflect the directions of the Second Vatican Council, but their own energy goes into family and work rather than parish renewal. As Kennedy insists, the Culture Two Catholics tend to see the Church as an extended family which remains their home despite the limitations of the leaders.

Rather than dismiss selective Catholics as disloyal, it would be better for Church leaders to take their experience seriously and to find more constructive ways to meet their needs. This in turn would promote a greater openness to Church authority which is needed for a balanced and integrated Christian life.

9. Reinvestigating Contemporary Catholicism

A bright young woman, who is reinvestigating her Catholic tradition after being out of the Church for years because of its repressive tendencies, reported this significant dream. In it, she visits a friend who takes her to the backyard of his home. There she is amazed to find a large Gothic cathedral. She is fascinated but is afraid to enter it. Overcoming her fears, she enters but soon discovers that it is only a facade with paper walls. Nevertheless, she remains fascinated and wants to stay within the walls, hoping to absorb from the open space a sense of peace and a feeling of transcendence. At some point, she is forced to leave the cathedral and experiences a tremendous sense of sadness as she realizes that it is not real and that she cannot return to it.

Social thinkers in the 19th and 20th centuries have helped us understand the fundamental ambivalence towards religion symbolized in the dream and experienced by many believers and non-believers. Early in the 19th century, the young philosopher Hegel (1770-1831) pointed out that traditional religion based on a God perceived as king and judge produced alienation in believers and helped to legitimate master-slave relationships in society. His disciple, Karl Marx (1818-1883), saw religion as an ideology which supports the inequities of the modern capitalistic system, and as an opiate which dulls believers' sense of current misery and injustice by turning their attention toward the future life of heaven. The influential French social philosopher August Comte (1798-1857) insisted that religion was an outmoded mythology which had to be replaced by scientific methods capable of producing a new humanity. Social thinkers in the 20th century have continued to point out the dehumanizing and oppressive tendencies of traditional religions. In doing so, they have articulated at least part of the experience of many Christians who report low self-esteem and a lack of confidence caused by doctrinaire and moralistic religious training. From this perspective, fear of reentering the cathedral is understandable.

On the other hand, social thinkers have also indicated positive ways in which religion functions. For example. Emile Durkheim (1858-1917), the French founder of modern sociology, though himself an atheist, understood religion positively as a symbolic celebration of the values, ideals and hopes that bind society together. He insisted that religion gives us a sense of belonging and helps contribute to the stability of society as a whole. Max Weber (1864-1920), a German sociologist, taught that religion provides us with a sense of meaning by detaching us from our egocentric needs and directing us to the good of the entire community. Karl Mannheim, in his important book *Ideology and Utopia*, pointed out that religion not only can be used to legitimate

the social order but also can play a liberating role by revealing the ills of society, undermining the authority of the ruling group and challenging the dominant value system.
Through the centuries, the Christian conviction that God will
destroy the old order and establish a new society has periodically fueled movements to reform the social order. Historically, the kingdom ideal preached by Jesus has played an
important role in moving individuals and groups to
challenge social sin and to transform the world.

This liberating and humanizing aspect of religion is
part of its continuing fascination. I do not doubt that entering the cathedral is an enticing option because it promises
an encounter with the deity leading to personal peace and
serenity. However, such an encounter, if authentic, should
promote human growth in all dimensions of life, including
the social. A comprehensive understanding of the positive
role of religion must include its inherent power to challenge
unjust structures and to promote a healthy institutional life
which enables human beings to flourish. A Gothic church
disconnected from everyday life inevitably becomes unreal.

Sociologists following Durkheim understand religion as
a symbol system. Thus the influential American sociologist
Robert Bellah has defined religion as "a set of symbolic
forms and acts that relate human beings to the ultimate conditions of their existence" (cf. *Habits of the Heart*). As theologian Gregory Baum, a great interpreter of the sociological
tradition, has reminded us, symbols are signs or images
which structure our consciousness and evoke emotions,
memories and dreams (cf. *Religion and Alienation* and *The Social Imperative*). Symbols are brought together in fundamental
stories or myths that reveal the hidden depths of life. These
symbols emerge in dreams, putting us in touch with the un-
conscious and revealing important patterns of human existence. Symbols structure our imagination, thereby affecting
the way we perceive our world. They form a grid through
which we view reality. They are so close to the core of our
being and so tightly woven into our consciousness that they
are hard to detect.

In the dream, the Gothic cathedral represents the traditional expression of the essential Catholic symbol system, while the illusory character of the structure suggests the diminished power of the older formulation to provide identity and meaning for people immersed in the patterns of the contemporary world. For some, the Gothic structure and all it represents remain fascinating and invite exploration. The danger is that it functions more like a museum than a living reality. Religious symbol systems constantly interact with the culture in which they exist. In times of great societal change, religions are forced to undergo radical transformations if they wish to survive. Some sociologists believe that Christianity has demonstrated its tremendous resilience and adaptive power by remaining an effective force in the United States with its pluralistic and democratic traditions. Since the Second Vatican Council, the Catholic community has been in a process of adapting the configuration and shape of its traditional symbols to the modern world. This is most evident in the liturgical changes, but also is involved in the efforts to restructure the institutional elements and to reinterpret dogmas and doctrines.

The dream suggests that the young woman knows at a deep level that the traditional expression of the Catholic symbol system, fascinating as it is, will not work for her as a way of interpreting her own experience and her place in the world. Her deep-seated sadness experienced in the dream may well be connected with the loss of a sense of belonging. The religion of her younger years may have been repressive, but it did give her a sense not only of identity, but also of a deeper meaning and purpose.

The significant question is whether the new configuration of the Catholic symbol system can meet her spiritual needs. In order to make it more attractive to her and other honest searchers, we must show that the contemporary expression of Catholicism can mediate a genuine relationship with the deity perceived as both imminent and transcendent. The diverse elements must be clearly related to Jesus Christ, the primary symbol who holds the system together and explicitly shares his risen life with the members. Andrew

Greeley has insisted that Catholics stay in the Church because they like being Catholic and appreciate the sacramental sense of God's presence in the world fostered by their religion. For people who have left the Church and are reinvestigating it, we must demonstrate that the contemporary expressions of the traditional symbols still attune us to the abiding presence of the Gracious Mystery in every aspect of human existence. In an attractive Catholic symbol system, the liturgy must still mediate an experience of the transcendent; traditional doctrines must have real meaning for everyday life; the social teaching must lead to effective action on behalf of peace and justice; and the whole package must be clearly centered on Jesus Christ.

My hope is that the young woman can find a constructive way of dealing with the ambivalent feelings triggered by the symbol of the Gothic cathedral. Perhaps she should find a vibrant Catholic community and gradually, without undue self-imposed pressure, begin to participate in its life and activities. In such a setting she may discover that the essential Catholic symbol system in its contemporary expression maintains a surprising power to satisfy her longings for identity and meaning.

What are we to learn from this dream experienced viewed through the lens of modern social thought? For those who find themselves wrestling with the transition from a traditional to a contemporary articulation of their religious tradition, it can provide a sense of solidarity and some guidance. For all of us, it invites a reexamination of the ways our religious symbol system shapes our consciousness and how responsive we are to its humanizing and liberating power.

10. Catholic Spirituality Since Vatican II

Since the Second Vatican Council ended more than 25 years ago, we have witnessed remarkable developments in the world of spirituality. These developments are in part a response to important societal changes, such as the migration to the suburbs, the environmental crisis, the growing gap between rich and poor and, more recently, the thaw in the Cold War. We have had to make sense out of Vietnam and Watergate, racism and sexism, street crime and drug addiction, all of which have helped shatter our utopian dreams. As the Catholic community has become more educated, we have become more critical of traditional forms of spirituality.

The liturgical changes unleashed by the Council have contributed to a more communal spirituality. Many persons have deepened their personal dedication to Christ and the gospel through their involvement in transparochial groups such as the Christian Family Movement, Marriage Encounter, Cursillo and the Charismatic Renewal, as well as parish-based programs such as RENEW. We have witnessed a remarkable growth in lay ministry, which has led to new efforts to develop a viable lay spirituality. Women, dissatisfied with the patriarchal structure of the Church, have sought new forms of spiritual nourishment, especially by participating with kindred spirits in faith-sharing groups.

Statistical surveys suggest that Catholics have changed their attitudes on many questions since the Council. For example, a high percentage are pleased with the greater participation in the new liturgy. More people are reading the Bible regularly. A large majority favors greater ecumenical involvement. Recently, Catholics have become more liberal on war and peace issues.

In the midst of all this change, an overwhelming majority of Catholics still feel that God loves them and that they have a close personal relationship with the Lord. They have no doubt that Jesus was fully God and fully human, and that he is still alive and active today. They find their nourishment and guidance in the liturgy so they can follow the law of love.

It might be helpful to map our own spiritual journey according to the following post-conciliar developments.

1) Contemporary Catholic spirituality continues to manifest the traditional ideal of unity in diversity. The pluralism

is evident and growing, as more and more Catholics feel free to choose among diverse life-style and pieties. Nevertheless, an essential unity in faith and religious sensibilities is still in place, even though it is harder to detect and define. The enduring challenge is to maintain a solid sense of Catholic unity based on fundamental beliefs and values which will encompass and support the expanding diversity.

2) Since the Council, the shape of Catholic piety has become simpler and clearer: more christocentric, more attuned to scriptural themes and more rooted in liturgical celebrations. Despite these developments, the Catholic imagination continues to be shaped by comforting images of Mary, the example of the saints and by certain popular devotions. For the future, we need a christocentric spirituality which focuses and expands the Catholic imagination so that it can appropriate the good example of virtuous people and the positive elements in popular piety.

3) Recently, Church leaders and spiritual guides have come to a deeper appreciation of the role of the parish in spiritual development. Vibrant parishes create a sense of community, facilitate personal growth and encourage efforts for justice and peace. It is difficult for parishioners to achieve sustained spiritual growth without this support and guidance. Still, the transparochial movements and groups continue to play an important role in meeting particular needs of Catholics. These groups will be more effective in the long run if they encourage and enable individuals to contribute to and draw on the resources of parish life.

4) The conciliar insistence on the universal call to holiness has made a great impact. A growing number of Catholics recognize that all the baptized, including laypersons, are called to live up to the highest ideals of the gospel. There is also a growing awareness that authentic discipleship must be practiced in the particular concrete circumstances of life. Thus, we face the great challenge of embodying the universal call to holiness in distinctive spiritualities which fit the needs and life-styles of laypersons, clergy and members of religious orders.

5) In the post-conciliar period, many Catholics have grown spiritually by participating in small groups which facilitate mutual sharing, personal witness and common prayer. Recently, spiritual leaders have become more aware of the dangers of privatism and the need to adopt a global perspective which includes collaborative efforts for the human good. The challenge for the future is to develop a global spirituality which encourages small faith-sharing groups to look beyond their own interests and to demonstrate an inclusive concern for the whole human family.

6) Since the Council, Catholicism has developed a solid incarnational spirituality which is attuned to finding God in the everyday world of human experience. At the same time, the contemporary world has generated new religious movements which stress striking religious experiences and esoteric private revelations. The continuing challenge for the Catholic world is to maintain a balanced spirituality which has a proper sense of the transcendence of God and provides an attractive alternative to spiritual fads.

7) Lay spirituality has continued to develop in two directions: one based on an ecclesiology of co-responsibility, which leads to involvement in the internal life of the Church; and another based on an understanding of the Church as instrument of the kingdom, which prompts efforts to humanize the political, economic and social spheres of life. The Church as a whole must find ways to balance and relate these two trends.

8) In the years since Vatican II, Catholic spirituality has expanded its array of truthful dialogue partners to include world religions, modern philosophies and humanities, and science. At the same time, the Catholic community has also reappropriated its own heritage, drawing on biblical insights, the teachings of the Fathers, the experiences of men and women mystics and the work of contemporary theologians. The enduring challenge is to develop a confident commitment to our own religious heritage which includes a fundamental openness to the truth, goodness and beauty found in other traditions and disciplines.

9) Contemporary feminist spirituality, rooted in the experiences of women, has instructed the whole Church in the destructive consequences of sexism and has expanded our perceptions of God and the process of salvation. Of late, it has also prompted initial efforts to develop a masculine spirituality which takes seriously the distinctive experience of men in our culture. Our task is to create an integral spirituality which draws on the experience of all people, promoting harmonious interactions between men and women based on mutuality and respect for their distinctive experiences.

10) Involved Catholics, often influenced by leaders such as Thomas Merton and Dorothy Day, have made important strides in creating a spirituality which is both prayerful and prophetic. Some have developed a rich inner life, which leads naturally to efforts on behalf of peace and justice. Others, working diligently to transform society, are thrown back upon the life of prayer for nourishment and strength. In the future, Catholic spirituality must maintain a fruitful tension between prayerful reflection and involvement in the world if it is to avoid falling into individualism or becoming a mere humanism. Catholic spirituality at its best encourages believers to find God in their hearts, as well as in worldly activities.

11. John Courtney Murray and Living Effectively in a Pluralistic Church

Since the Second Vatican Council, we have become more aware of the pluralism which exists in the Catholic community. Conservatives and liberals have found themselves disagreeing about many issues, ranging from birth control and in vitro fertilization to the position of the United States bishops on peace and the economy. Unfortunately, the polarization seems to be growing, and the debate is taking on a harsher tone. Reasoned argument is often replaced by emotional outbursts. Some passionate critics resort to personal attacks in their zeal to refute the errors of their opponents. Individuals who claim a monopoly on the truth speak as though they have the right to decide who is in and out of the Church.

This harsh rhetoric, which can be heard on both sides of the current debate, ignores the New Testament mandate that Christians should live in peace and harmony. Bickering within the Church diminishes its power to accomplish good in the world. The strategy of personal attacks does not reflect the approach and style of Jesus. The demand for uniformity in thought and practice undercuts the traditional Catholic ideal of unity in diversity.

In this situation, it may be helpful for all concerned to look once again at John Courtney Murray, S.J., the most influential theologian yet produced in the United States. Murray is especially helpful because he is admired and claimed by both liberals and neo-conservatives. Both sides tend to think of themselves as carrying on his project and being faithful to his legacy. Neo-conservatives like to point to Murray's obvious loyalty to the Church, represented by his obedient acceptance of the Vatican command in 1955 to cease writing and speaking about religious liberty. They also admire his great respect for the Catholic heritage, as well as his insistence that the Catholic community has a special role to play in revitalizing American public life. On the other hand, those of us with a liberal bent highlight his great accomplishment in bringing the distinctive American experience of religious liberty into the consciousness of the whole Church.

Since both conservatives and liberals have a fundamental respect for John Courtney Murray, perhaps he can instruct all of us on the importance of civil discourse and constructive dialogue as a means of living effectively in a pluralistic situation. Although Murray expressed his views on civil discourse in a political context, some of his ideas do have application to the world of the Church as well. Thus, following his line of thought, we can say that the life of the faith community is enhanced when believers are "locked together in argument" and are passionately engaged in reasonable discussion of the ways of expressing and practicing the faith.

In the Catholic community, we should be able to live in "emotional solidarity" because of our shared history and our fundamental beliefs and values. We do have a common Catholic imagination, which is focused on positive images of God and Christ. As Catholics, we have common sensibilities, shaped by our regular participation in the Eucharist and by our membership in a Church with a long tradition and a universal appeal. We naturally turn to the sacraments as a fitting way of celebrating the great events in life and of meeting our spiritual needs.

With his strong intellectual bent, Murray insisted that constructive argument among responsible people is the way to deepen self-understanding and to create a more harmonious community. The health of the Church depends on informed believers discussing openly, honestly and charitably their different perceptions of the fundamental truths and values of the faith. But such open conversations are possible only on the basis of mutual trust. The practice of imputing bad will to those who disagree or of attributing their particular opinions to a lack of moral rectitude poisons the life of the Church precisely because it undercuts the very possibility of honest dialogue.

Furthermore, Murray held that constructive conversations require a common language, initial points of agreement and a core of commonly-held truths. He pointed out that we can argue constructively only within a context of fundamental agreement. It seems important for Catholics who disagree to search out that kind of common ground.

There is no doubt that we share most fundamental convictions: the belief in a provident, triune God who lavishes his love upon us; the conviction that Jesus Christ is the Son of God, the final prophet and the absolute savior; and the belief that the Holy Spirit continues to be active in our hearts and in our world today. We believe that the Church is the sacrament of the Risen Christ and functions as the sign and instrument of the kingdom in the world. The Eucharist remains central for all of us, as does following the law of the love of God and neighbor, which leads to the final fulfillment of heaven.

Within this context of fundamental agreement, we have the opportunity to argue charitably and constructively about diverse formulations and applications of the common faith, as well as about more peripheral questions.

Murray feared the "modern-day barbarians" who reject the role of reason in public affairs and who resort to the rule of force and fear. Barbarians replace dialogue with monologue, reason with passion, and civility with harsh rhetoric. They think they have an exclusive hold on the truth and feel called to convert or coerce others to their way of thinking. Barbarians make conversation impossible. Murray's warning against political barbarians can well be applied to those who are poisoning the discussion within the Church today.

Murray had profound insights into the psychological factors which preclude genuine dialogue. He spoke about the "structures of passion and war," which include hidden resentments and a profound distrust of those who hold a different worldview. Dialogue and cooperation are possible only if these hidden motivations are brought to light and discussed openly. Within the Church today, the differences of opinion on particular issues often flow from very different mindsets or fundamental perceptions of reality. For example, people who view the world from a static viewpoint and in fixed categories find it most difficult to understand those with an evolutionary mindset. Unfortunately, this lack of understanding can also include hidden resentments and a fundamental distrust. When this is the case, the structures of passion and war take over and harsh rhetoric replaces civil discourse.

It seems that only Christian charity can overcome this fundamental difficulty. We need the help of the Spirit in order to love and respect those fellow believers with whom we have fundamental disagreements. We must learn to see Christ not only in Buddhists and Hindus but also in fellow Catholics. Charity requires the perspective of faith which enables us to see the other as a dialogue partner, rather than a subtle enemy.

The traditional Catholic wisdom is that in essential matters we should have unity; in accidental matters, we should enjoy freedom; and in all things, we should maintain charity. John Courtney Murray is a modern example of that traditional wisdom. By word and example, he challenges both conservatives and liberals to maintain civil discourse and to cultivate the life of charity as a basis for building up the Church, the Body of Christ.

12. The Spiritual Search and the Catholic Religion

Dear Sue,

This is a response to your long letter and our recent extended conversation which continues to intrigue me. It is not often that I talk to someone who has read my book *Apologetics and the Eclipse of Mystery* so thoroughly, and informs me that I missed a particular German volume in my bibliography. Your spiritual journey is a fascinating one. Eighteen years is a long time to be away from the Church, especially for a person who attended Catholic grade school and high school. Your renewed interest in religious affairs seems most important to me and well worth pursuing. I hope my responses to some of your questions will lead to further reflection on your part and continued dialogue.

I think it is important to start with the "inclinations" which have been stirring in your heart for about eight years now. Your descriptions of an intense longing for silence, a deep desire for internal peace, a profound appreciation for the beauty, power and wonder of nature and a continuing love for music, art and literature strike me as manifestations of your essentially religious nature. It seems to me you are getting in touch with the deeper dimensions of your being which cannot be satisfied by material possessions or exhausted by rational analysis. That is why I said it was not hard for me to interpret your journey as prompted by the Spirit, the very source of our internal dynamism. My mentor, Karl Rahner, insisted that we need not consider every person who leaves the Church and then returns as one more exemplification of the prodigal son story. I am not sure where your current inquiry will take you, but I know I have great respect for the authenticity and integrity of your spiritual journey to this point. My sense is that you have deep and refined religious sensibilities which will not let you settle for the superficiality fostered by our fast-paced, consumerist culture. Perhaps you are indeed being pursued by the "Hound of Heaven." In my opinion, it is not healthy for you to repress or ignore these longings. It is better to pay attention to them, to seek out their source and to discern where they are leading you. Your current intense and sometimes painful quest reminds me of Augustine's famous description of "the restless heart" and Rahner's suggestion that we human beings have a question mark at the very center of our being. My hope is that your continuing quest is a rewarding, if challenging, adventure undertaken with confidence that the very journey itself has intrinsic meaning.

Your own phrase, "a sensuous experience of God," strikes me as an excellent way of describing your deeper inclinations. It certainly does not brand you as a heathen, as you feared I would think. Even though you have such a fine analytical mind with a penchant for clear rational arguments, I believe you should take these sensuous experiences as the starting point of your religious quest. In everyday life, we trust certain experiences without being able to explain them completely. We know certain things are true, even when we cannot convince others of this fact. Reason does not ground these experiences, but rather illuminates and guides them. It is not as though we use our logical powers to establish a certain position and then commit ourselves to it. On the contrary, we find ourselves with certain convictions and fundamental outlooks which can then be analyzed in greater depth.

Your sensuous experiences have an authenticity about them because they accord with your primary ways of experiencing the world and with the poetic and imaginative aspect of your personality. They provide a great foundation point for your continuing spiritual quest. After all, the Christian faith proclaims that God is definitely revealed in a man who walked this hard earth, shed real tears, worked with his hands, provided wine for a party, admired the flowers of the field, sweat blood and loved his friends. Surely such a religion can affirm and encourage the revelatory power of sensuous experiences. As I see it, your real problem is to find a symbol system which can illumine and direct your sensuous longings. Now that your deeper drives have invaded your conscious awareness, you are experiencing a need to understand and express them. I presume that is why you were intrigued by the sentence in my book which indicates that our deeper awareness "always and necessarily objectifies itself in various degrees ranging from vague mood through initial reflection, verbalization, symbolic expression and external action." It is the symbolic expression which is crucial, as your intuition has already suggested to you. That must be why you were so fascinated by Joseph Campbell's book *Myths to Live By*. Campbell's traditional Catholic background shows through when he speaks about the power of dramatic rituals, employing symbols such as the crucifix, incense and Gregorian chant to product a positive "affect image" and to reveal the eternal God. His point is well taken that symbol and ritual speak directly to the "feeling system," producing a "throb of resonance" and uniting individuals in "one spiritual organism."

This analysis of the way symbols function is crucial to the next phase of your spiritual journey. You must find a symbol system which resonates with your deepest inclinations. In this regard, I was intrigued by your comment that you "love being in old churches" because it brings a sense of peace and belonging, but that at Mass you are pressured to believe, to participate and "to be someone you are not."

This not only reinforces my conviction that you need some sort of explicit religious expression, but also suggests that you are still encumbered by an outmoded understanding of the Catholic symbol system which still produces such negative "affect images" in you.

I realize that your current search may lead you to investigate alternative symbol systems, such as Eastern religions or the Quaker tradition. It will be important for you, however, to include a reinvestigation of your Catholic heritage as part of the process. When you do, you will need to make sure you have thoroughly "deliteralized" the traditional Catholic symbols. This means that all of the institutional elements which comprise the Catholic heritage, including scriptures, creeds, dogmas, doctrines, sacraments and devotions, function not as literal portrayals of divine activities, but as symbolic pointers to a Mystery which remains inexhaustible. The doctrine of the Ascension, for example, does not mean that Christ went up in the sky; nor does talk of the fatherhood of God mean that God is male. I am stressing this precisely because Joseph Campbell has often failed to apply this fundamental truth in his comments on Christian dogmas and doctrines. In one of the passages you cited, for example, he simply assumes that dogmas are merely rational ways of conceptualizing symbols. Thus he misses their deeper function of pointing out particular aspects of the great Mystery. I believe you will get a more accurate picture of your Catholic heritage if you see it as a comprehensive symbol system which illumines the deepest questions of life and guides us on the journey. Catholicism is a global vision, a complete worldview, a total way of life which touches our minds and hearts through myth, symbol and ritual. Furthermore, it is impossible to ask and solve every individual question about its truth claims. It is possible to see if the symbol system as a whole meets your real needs by helping you to achieve a deeper understanding of your sensuous experiences of God and to respond better to the divine summons.

Within that framework, reinterpretation of the individual doctrines and rituals which comprise the Catholic symbol system will be helpful. You need a contemporary way of understanding, for instance, the meaning of the redemption and power of the Eucharist. It will be important to find out why you are uncomfortable at Mass and to see if new perspectives on the Eucharist will help. All of this will take study and some experimentation. Perhaps you could go to Mass and just sit in the back, without even trying to participate. As to the studies, I will be happy to offer guidance along the way. In the meantime, I want you to know that I have great respect for your current quest and believe that the Spirit is with you in the process.

13. The Catholic Church and Free-Thinking Inquirers

Michael, a perceptive and insightful young man, is thinking of joining the Catholic community. He grew up in a Unitarian family which prided itself on being open to various religious traditions. His mother made sure that he had some acquaintance with Buddhism, Hinduism, Judaism and Islam, in addition to Christianity. He was taught that there were many paths to God, and that religious tolerance was a virtue to be prized. Eventually, his parents adopted a totally humanistic outlook on life, severing even their tenuous connections with the Unitarian Church.

As a result of his upbringing, Michael was never really involved in a religious tradition as a participant. He was acquainted with various religions, but always as a casual observer without a serious commitment. When he went away to college, he did not undergo the typical crisis of faith experienced by many of his friends, who grew up immersed in a particular religion. For them, campus life challenged their assumptions and broadened their horizons. The openness of the university struck them as liberating compared to the more restrictive atmosphere created by family and Church back home. The collegiate experience forced them out of the narrow religious world with all of its apparent certainties into a broader world of questioning and doubt.

Michael's collegiate experience was very different. The openness and tolerance of university life was quite familiar to him and generally comfortable. The unfamiliar appeared when he interacted closely with newfound friends, who were mostly Catholics. They seemed to have something he did not have. At first, he could not identify it but did find it fascinating. As he got to know these friends better, he realized that they all came from a defined world, were molded by a particular tradition and had similar experiences, which gave them a common outlook. Even those who were in rebellion against their religious heritage had something definite to define themselves against. When they made jokes about their repressive training, they were still expressing in another way their common bonding. Even the anger expressed by some indicated the importance they attached to their religious background. What they had that he did not was a genuine engagement with religious tradition. While he had observed religion from the outside, they had experienced it from the inside. This experience fascinated him but also frightened him. Catholicism was intriguing, but it appeared to be excessively restrictive and closed, especially to a person who had grown up with a spirit of religious tolerance.

As we were discussing these matters, he suddenly recalled another major part of his life story. From his earliest years, he had loved music and had shown promise as a musician. His mother felt he had natural talent and was convinced he would excel because of his creative and spontaneous spirit. In order to pursue his interest, Michael went to the university to study music. As he did his course work and studied music theory, he seemed to lose his spontaneity and creativity. His performances became labored and mechanical. His mother, who highly treasured freedom of expression, blamed her son's disappointing progress on the music department, which put excessive emphasis on theory, and on professors, who employed extremely rigid approaches.

As Michael now reflects on his mother's analysis, he is really not sure if he still agrees with it or not. There is another side to the story. Music theory has proven not only necessary but valuable for his career as a music teacher. The disciplined work required by his best teachers has enhanced his skills and given him a model for his own teaching. On good days, he feels some of his creativity and spontaneity returning. As the years go on, he finds greater value in the musical education he received.

There was, of course, no mystery why this aspect of his life jumped into his consciousness as we were talking about his joining the Catholic community. Clearly he fears that joining the Church will be a repetition of the negative aspects of his collegiate experience. He envisions harsh disciplines, which will cramp his spirit, and strict teachings, which will constrain his inquiring mind. He is not sure he wants his children living in the restricted and heavy world of Catholicism, as depicted by the many stories he heard from his Catholic friends. The free and spontaneous world created by his family still has great appeal for him.

His feelings, however, are clearly mixed. Just as he can see a more positive side to his rigorous musical training, so he can sense the potential value in being a committed member of a Church with definite teachings and rules. Total freedom can produce a certain dizziness—an anxiety over multiple options. Perhaps joining the Catholic community could offer him a sense of stability and rootedness, which have been missing in his life. Part of him thinks that it would be healthy for his children to grow up knowing at least one religion from the inside. He would, of course, want them to be open-minded and to know about other religions. The question he poses to himself is whether joining the Church will be liberating or restrictive. Will commitment to a particular religion damage his free spirit or, on the contrary, will it release a new creativity? Can Catholicism provide an overarching structure, which will help him understand and live out his innate tolerance in a more constructive way?

For Michael, there will be no simple answers to these complex questions. Given his background, he will join the Church only if it accords with his deepest longings and promises to be beneficial for himself and those he loves.

While Michael's sharply-etched story is not typical, it is important because it represents a growing challenge to the Church. Since the Council, the Catholic community has worked hard to enable individual members to move from a narrow, restricted understanding of Christianity to a more universal and tolerant outlook. We obviously must continue this work with vigor and intelligence.

At the same time, we must also recognize the new situation represented by Michael. In our culture, an increasing number of youngsters grow up in religiously-amorphous families, lacking any genuine commitment to a particular religious tradition. The religious pluralism which we practice in our society can also lead to religious indifference. Even in Catholic circles, the emphasis on tolerance and openness can produce the "marshmallow effect" in which young people have no clear teaching or precise guidelines against which they can define themselves. Catholicism can become so fragmented and diffuse that it no longer creates a distinctive world. We can envision some circles in which jokes about Catholic rigidity are no longer intelligible, let alone funny.

In this changing situation, we can expect more people to follow the path traveled by Michael. Their movement will be from the universal to the particular, from a vague acquaintance with religion to a definite commitment. They will be looking for a solid tradition, which provides roots and clear teaching, which offers guidance.

We must find healthy ways of responding to the needs of these people. No doubt some of them will be tempted by the simple answers and cheap grace promised by Christian groups with exclusivist tendencies. This approach, however, not only falsifies the Christian message, but it fails to meet the real needs of contemporary inquirers. They need a Christian community which, at the same time, calls for a serious commitment and remains open to God's trust and goodness manifested throughout the world. The faith community should mediate to them the rich and diverse Christian tradition, with all its wisdom and inspiration for dealing with the unavoidable complexities of contemporary life. These new inquirers are not vitally concerned with the struggles for religious tolerance, which have engaged so many of us since before and after the Second Vatican Council. Their real concern is to find a mature, vibrant faith community, which provides motivation and resources for living in today's world with commitment and tolerance.

14. The Nature of Catholicism and Reactions to the Pope

We can learn important lessons about the nature of Catholicism by reflecting on the reaction of Catholics to the Pope. The visit of John Paul II to the United States in 1987 exemplifies the point because his presence produced such intense and diverse reactions, ranging from uncritical enthusiasm to angry resentments. A priest friend of mine, who combines love of the Church with a healthy sense of the limitations of the hierarchy, serves as a good example of those who responded in a fundamentally positive way to the papal visit. Before the visit he had many negative feelings, fearing papal authoritarianism and deploring the media hype. When the Pope actually arrived, he watched a bit of it on TV and found himself getting more involved in the opening events. The momentum built and he became more enthusiastic about the Pope's presence as the days went on. He liked the structure of the dialogue that was set up and was proud of the way that the laypeople, sisters, priests and bishops tried to represent the thinking of American Catholics to the Pope. The large gatherings for liturgy led by the Pope gave him a deeper sense of what it means to be Catholic, producing within him a sense of pride in his religion. Seeing so many diverse people brought into unity by the eucharistic celebrations moved him deeply, giving him a vague sense of what the kingdom might be all about. The Pope, of course, said some things with which he disagreed, but this aspect of the papal visit seemed less important than the sense of solidarity established among the 52 million Catholics in the United States.

On the other hand, a liberal Catholic laywoman explained to me that she found almost everything about the papal visit to be offensive. She did not like the media hype, the money spent, the TV coverage, the emphasis put on the papal image and the failure of the official spokespersons to express their case more vigorously. Her anger intensified when the Pope responded to those who were looking for genuine dialogue by repeating his harsh and rigid positions on the internal Church matters, such as birth control and divorce. The last straw for her came when the Pope insisted to the Catholic bishops that dissent is not compatible with being a "good Catholic."

In between these clear-cut positions, many people experienced ambivalent responses to the Pope and his message. Andrew Greeley, for example, spoke for many liberal Catholics when he said "people like the singer but not the song." Thus, people were taken with the Pope's charismatic personality and brilliant intellect, while strenuously objecting to his rigid stand on questions such as birth control. On the conservative side, William Buckley was impressed with the Pope's spiritual integrity, which enabled him, for example, to reject the popular enthusiasm for abortion. On the other hand, Buckley suggested that when we consider the Holy Father's comments about the sanctuary movement or economic questions, we should remind ourselves of the many fields in which he is fallible. Moreover, he seemed to suggest that people simply not listen to the Pope on these questions. While conservatives are tuning out the Pope's message on social questions, many liberals ignore his teachings on sexual matters, such as divorce and remarriage. Some commentators have called this a "cafeteria approach to Catholicism," insisting that good Catholics should accept everything that the Pope has to say.

There are, of course, many ways of analyzing the varied responses of Catholics to the Pope and his message. It would be interesting, for example, to compare Pope John Paul II with former President Reagan, who provided a sense of security and well-being, even to some who disagreed with his specific policies. Tempting as that line of thought might be, I would like to analyze the varied responses from the viewpoint of the nature and function of religion.

As the sociologists remind us, religions are symbol systems or interpretive schemes which give an over-arching meaning to life and provide a total way of living. Religions have many components, such as doctrines, creeds, liturgical actions, moral precepts, theologies, spiritualities and institutional elements. At the same time, all of these components are joined together by a set of core beliefs which guide a consistent and coherent way of living in the world.

Applying these general notions, Catholicism also appears as a comprehensive, integrated package. It is a complete way of being human and of relating to ourselves, our interpersonal world and our God. Moreover, Catholicism is an extremely rich symbol system. We can think for example, of the Nicene Creed, Marian doctrines, eucharistic celebrations, Lenten ashes, monastic spirituality, classical and contemporary theology, struggles for peace and justice and hierarchical leadership. Not everything in the package is of equal importance. There is a proper hierarchy of truths and actions. The practice of charity, for instance, is more important than speaking in tongues. Commitment to Christ is essential, while devotion to the saints is not. Easter has greater significance than the Assumption. The command of Jesus to love our enemies carries greater weight than the papal prohibition of birth control.

Furthermore, Catholicism is an organic, interpretive scheme. The various components do not exist in isolation, but draw their meaning and strength from their relationship to the core message. The central message of Catholicism can be expressed in various ways. We can speak, for instance, about commitment to Jesus Christ as the final prophet and the absolute savior, or we can affirm that the absolute mystery in rule over our lives is revealed as trustworthy in and through Jesus Christ. However we express it, the core of Catholicism has to do with our personal relationship to Jesus Christ. The following of Christ must issue in a life of charity. The other elements in the Catholic symbol system not only derive their meaning from the core message, but also should intensity and fructify this central relationship to Christ.

No one can totally appropriate in an existential way all of the various elements in the Catholic symbol system. Individuals, for example, might draw strength for their daily life from devotion to the Sacred Heart but find no real spiritual help from the doctrine of hell. Some people find that they get a great deal out of the Good Friday service and derive little benefit from the Easter Vigil. Matthew's Gospel may be illuminating to a particular person, while the letters of Paul simply do not speak to the heart. In this sense, all of us, the hierarchy included, are selective Catholics. Some elements of the symbol system appeal to us more than others. Everyone ignores some components of the interpretive scheme almost entirely. The requirement for being Catholic is not that we find great spiritual relevance in absolutely every teaching and practice in Catholicism, but that we stay open to the possibility that the essential doctrines and practices have a potential power to illumine and inspire human life. In summary, Catholicism guides and inspires its adherents, not so much by its individual points of doctrine and morality, but rather as a comprehensive unified system of beliefs and actions. We say that it works for us as a whole, helping us to understand the deepest questions of life and motivating us to live more responsibly.

This understanding of the Catholic symbol system may help explain some of the diverse reactions to the papal visit. For those who responded positively, the Pope somehow articulated the core of the Catholic understanding of life. Perhaps he represented the unity of the whole community or the compassionate caring aspect of following Christ or the fundamental responsibilities involved in living out the gospel. In other words, he pushed the right buttons which activated the power of the total package. He helped people perceive Catholicism as an effective and powerful way of being human and of relating to the world. I suspect that the positive reaction of many people of other religious backgrounds is connected with this sense of Catholicism portrayed by the Pope.

For others, the Pope clearly pushed the wrong buttons. He seemed to focus on the peripheral elements in Catholicism, rather than its core. They heard the emphasis on the disciplinary laws, such as mandatory celibacy and the prohibition against women priests, which have little to do with the essential challenge of following Christ. For them, the Pope did not really demonstrate the power of the faith as they know it but rather presented it in a weakened form by emphasizing non-essentials. Even worse, by denying all possibility of dissent, the Pope seemed to rob them of their adult responsibility to understand their faith as a whole and to make it their own. In short, they were disappointed and frustrated by the Pope's visit because his rigid stands on peripheral matters obscured for them the unity, coherence and beauty of the Catholic faith as they know it.

Finally, this analysis of Catholicism suggests that from one perspective we are all "cafeteria Catholics." We all inevitably select aspects of the faith that illumine and inspire our daily lives. It would seem important to do this intelligently and critically while remaining open to the wisdom found in the Church as a whole.

Chapter Three

Improving Ministry and Liturgy

1. An Anniversary Reflection on Priesthood

An important anniversary of my ordination to the priesthood is approaching. Various responses suggest themselves:

I could follow the promptings of my reticent nature and ignore the whole thing. But this would effectively deny the public character of the priesthood and may offend the sensibilities of the many people who have enriched my life as a priest.

I could write a carefully-worded theological explanation of the priesthood, noting the contemporary shift from the cultic model of the priest as a unique, privileged figure who functions as a mediator to the servant/leader model which sees the priest as a member of the faith community charged with proclaiming the Word of God. This approach, however, may be heavier than the occasion warrants.

I could make an impassioned plea for voluntary celibacy, based on the harm done by the current law and the potential value of a married clergy. But such a discussion could overwhelm other more important issues.

I could tell some stories (many probably exaggerated by now) of exciting moments—like the time a young woman with a gun appeared in my office, threatening suicide. Highlighting such dramatic moments, however, would surely give a distorted view of a life most often immersed in the ordinary.

I could publicly confess limitations, transgressions, sins, and tarnished ideals. But this might squander important material better saved for my future novel about a young man who desperately wanted to be a major league baseball player but who became a priest when he finally realized he could neither field nor hit.

I could reflect, with a mixed sense of failure and hope, on the many people who deserved better service from me than they got: the alcoholic sleeping in an abandoned dwelling who received food periodically but no long-term help; the couple struggling with birth control who received nothing but the official teaching; the young fundamentalist who received an intellectual challenge but little compassion. Despite the potential value of exploring ministerial failures, my decision is to postpone such healing reflections for another time.

Instead, I intend to celebrate this anniversary by recalling the ways the Mystery has manifested itself to me as *gracious* during my years as a leader in the faith community. My life has been filled with signals of transcendence, signs of hope and intimations of mystery.

Individually, these manifestations remain ambiguous, defying clear and conclusive interpretations. Together, they suggest—at least to me—that my ministry has some sort of ultimate meaning despite all the darkness which has surrounded it. This faith conviction can be expressed in various ways: My efforts have not been wasted. My shortcomings are not the last word. My ministry is part of a larger project which will ultimately succeed. In other words, the Holy Spirit has been at work supplying for weaknesses, gathering into unity fragmented efforts and insuring the ultimate significance of partial successes.

The ministry of leadership has been kinder to me than I ever anticipated. The dark forebodings which marked my preparation time in the seminary fortunately disappeared in the actual practice of serving the community. The ministry has remained a challenge, functioning as a catalyst for my own personal development. Interactions with parishioners have helped me overcome my innate shyness, teaching me to deal with a wide variety of persons. The challenge of teaching and preaching has prompted regular reflection and continued education. The ministry has afforded me marvelous opportunities to study under some of the world's best theologians. This, in turn, has improved the quality of my work and intensified my sense of responsibility to share what I have learned with others. Finally, the role of leadership has thrust me into situations and provided forums in which I have been able to speak and act on behalf of peace and justice. While these efforts have been limited, they have enabled me to express my innate sense of compassion in a constructive way.

Throughout my years of service, I have had an abiding sense that the ministry is intrinsically worthwhile. My conviction is that a hardened and fragmented world needs the Christian message of reconciliation and hope. The community of faith needs leadership which can orchestrate the talents and gifts of all of its members. Individuals and society as a whole need visible reminders that it is possible for human beings to live in peace and harmony, working for the common good in a cooperative way.

For me, the value of ministerial service is rooted in the presence of the Mystery which gives deeper meaning to all of our human activities. When my eyes of faith are properly focused, they do indeed discern the presence of the Spirit in all of these ministerial challenges and opportunities.

This is not to deny the burdensome character of this type of ministry. It has been hard work. Not the kind of tiresome toil known by many laborers; not the kind of continuous demand experienced by mothers of small children; not the kind of exhausting routine common to workers who have little control over their time; not the kind of pressure encountered by those struggling to move up the socioeconomic ladder—but the ministry is demanding and fatiguing in its own way!

The challenge is to be present to people despite distractions, to remain open despite misunderstandings, to get primed for liturgies despite their frequency, to teach with zest despite fatigue, to work for peace and justice despite limited success, to write despite personal limitations, to be a public person despite a desire for privacy, to hold the community together despite divisions, and to pray despite time demands. Over the years the demands have multiplied as new projects begin and more people exercise their claims on my time and energy. Exalted language which speaks of "a special vocation" and "a joyful love of priestly ministry" does not come easily to my lips. I am more comfortable in saying that my work is pressurized but at times enjoyable, demanding but often rewarding, difficult but generally worthwhile.

Reflection on my many years of ministerial service—from my first parish to my current assignment as a campus minister—reveals the Mystery which brings order out of chaos and life out of death. My beginning years at St. Mary's Parish in Sandusky were one vast learning experience. It's hard to imagine being more poorly prepared for the challenging work of serving the real needs of parishioners. The theology taught in the seminary did not help much in the pulpit or classroom. Years of isolation in the seminary did little to enhance interpersonal skills. Nonetheless, the parishioners were surprisingly patient and respectful. The lay leaders in the parish indirectly instructed me in the meaning of priestly service by taking the initiative and making suggestions for new approaches and programs. Long hours of listening in Christian Family Movement meetings, where priests were not allowed to speak, acquainted me with the concerns and aspirations of married people. Interaction with parishioners tended to confirm the lessons of sober realism and self-acceptance instilled in me by my parents.

My contributions to the life of St. Mary's Parish flowed from my intuitive sense of the meaning of the changes signaled by the Second Vatican Council. I spoke continuously of the need and potential value of reform in the Church. Those were heady days when those of us who worked side by side to make reform real at the local level formed special bonds. For me, talk about the presence of the Lord became real in and through those good people.

That perception has set the tone for my ministry ever since. Further studies, new ministerial challenges and the opportunities to write—all have been enriched by this fundamental experience.

Wherever my ministry has taken me since then—Mount St. Mary Seminary in Cincinnati, St. Thomas More University Parish in Bowling Green and Corpus Christi in Toledo— I have encountered generous persons committed to living out the gospel in real-life situations. My memory is filled with examples: young persons who maintained high ideals despite peer pressures; seminarians who worked with intelligence and courage to improve their course of studies; married couples who dedicated themselves to raising their children; single persons who contributed significantly to the common good; friends from other religious and humanistic traditions who combined commitment and tolerance; sisters who led the way in Church renewal; and priests who functioned as genuine leaders of the community.

These individuals are not idealized abstractions for me but have definite names and specific faces. They are not perfect, but they do exemplify particular virtues. To let their faces play before my imagination is to feel a quiet joy and a deep sense of appreciation. They appear to me as undeserved gifts who have brought stability and zest to my years as a priest. My gratitude runs deep indeed because through these good people, I have learned something of what it means to say that the Mystery is both trustworthy and gracious.

2. A New Model of Priesthood: Leader and Member

Functioning as a priest in today's Church provides a distinctive set of challenges. As older priests commonly observe, they were trained in the seminary for one type of ministry but somewhere along the line all the rules changed. Suddenly their priestly life took on a very different form. Some priests have had a great deal of difficulty adjusting to this new ministerial situation. They find themselves pining for the good old days when the pastor enjoyed the unquestioning respect of his people and could unilaterally shape the vision and direction of the parish.

Many laypeople have also experienced difficulties in trying to relate to the clergy in the new ways suggested by the Second Vatican Council. They often are not clear on precisely what they can and should expect from their priests. Nor do they know the best ways to support the clergy they see groping for a viable identity.

These tensions and confusions over the role of the priest in the contemporary Catholic Church are inevitable. We are passing through a transition period in which the still dominant cultic model of the priest as "mediator" is being challenged and gradually replaced by the less well-defined model of the priest as "leader" of the faith community.

The popular version of the cultic model is very familiar to us. It emphasizes the priest's unique privilege and duty, shared by no one else in the community, to offer the sacrifice of the Mass, to hear confessions and to anoint the sick. Through the laying on of the bishop's hands in ordination, a man is marked by a special character as a representative of the Lord in the Church. The priest enjoys great respect as a mediator between God and the members of the community. He is expected to live a celibate life-style which distinguishes him from most people in the community but which also frees him to serve the needs of all. A good deal of the priest's significance and personal satisfaction derives from his presence at the great sacramental occasions, such as

Baptisms, First Communions, conversions which are ritualized in Confession, marriage and the anointing of the seriously ill.

Unfortunately, the cultic model tends to produce a clerical caste system in which priests adopt authoritarian and individualistic approaches to ministry. At its best, however, this model guides priests into generous service which enriches the life of the community.

According to a survey conducted by the National Conference of Diocesan Vocation Directors a couple of years ago, over 58 percent of respondents (including laity, vowed religious and priests from all over the country) said that this cultic model was operative in the majority of priests in their diocese. Only 16 percent thought that the model of priest as "leader" of the faith community was the dominant model.

When these same respondents were asked about their hopes for the future, however, the results changed dramatically. Around 85 percent wanted priests to function as leaders of their faith community. Only 32 percent listed the cultic model in their top choices. The obvious disparity between actual priestly practice and the hopes of many for a new model of priesthood helps to explain many of the tensions in the Church today.

While the new model is still in the process of being formed, certain trends are clear. A shift is occurring, for example, away from the emphasis on the uniqueness of the ordained priesthood toward an inclusive understanding of the priest as a leader who shares in the common life of the faith community. The cultic model, by stressing the priest's special liturgical functions and celibate life-style, tends to isolate him from the real concerns of others, especially the heavy responsibility and dominating concern of raising children. When parishioners place the priest on a pedestal, he tends to function as a somewhat remote authoritarian figure. The cultic model calls the priest to live a life of holiness but shields him from the harshness and routine endured by others. It demands a life of self-sacrifice but grants the priest high respect and special privileges.

A growing resistance to this isolating aspect of the cultic model of the priesthood can be detected among both laity and clergy. Some parishioners harbor resentments, both hidden and apparent, over the privileged status of priests which absolve them from the burdens and responsibilities borne by laypeople. Others simply want to relate to priests as individual persons who share fully in the human adventure. While maintaining a fundamental respect for the priesthood, they reject the notion that priests are inherently holier than laypersons. They tend to judge individual priests according to their personal qualities and ministerial skills. In their minds, priests should be just as accountable as other responsible persons in the community.

Many priests today are also dissatisfied with the cultic model and are searching for a new model of priesthood. They are trying to work out healthier ways of relating to the people they serve. They are uncomfortable with signs of uniqueness and special clerical privilege which isolate them from the laity. They want to be respected for who they are and the services they perform rather than for the role they play. These priests want to lead their parishes not by imposing their will but by empowering others to take up their proper responsibilities in the Church.

The New Testament supports the current effort to establish greater equality, mutuality and collaboration between priests and laity. Jesus of Nazareth, a layman who preached more about ordinary life and the building of the kingdom than about ritual sacrifice and temple worship, shared in the life of the people he served. He broke down the barriers separating groups and individuals. He revealed his deepest anxieties and longings to the inner circle of disciples whom he called his friends. His death and resurrection brought an outpouring of the Spirit which gathered his followers, forming them into a community.

These followers become convinced that all baptized persons share in the priesthood of Christ (1 Peter 2:9) and receive charisms, or free gifts of the Spirit, which are to be used to build up the Body of Christ (1 Corinthians 12:7). The charism of leadership does not give a special status or privileged position; but it does impose the responsibility to oversee the community and care for the needs of the members. Following the example and teaching of Jesus, leaders are to function not as authoritarians but as *servants* (Mark 10:42-45). In other words, priestly life rooted in the Scriptures is characterized more by foot-washing than by pedestal-sitting.

My personal response to this period of transition was, at first, to concentrate on living a life of service while suspending discussions of the unique identity and special functions connected with the priesthood. The private soul-searching and public discussion of the role of the priest in those years after the Council struck me as self-serving and counterproductive.

Now, however, circumstances such as the priest shortage, along with developments in "postmodern theology," have forced me and many others to reconsider what is unique about the priesthood. My own sense is that serious Christians today want priests to be not only friends but also spiritual leaders, not only fellow searchers but also wise guides, not only participants in secular life but also shapers of the liturgical world. Perhaps we could borrow a notion from the philosopher A. N. Whitehead and begin to speak about the "inclusive uniqueness" of the priesthood.

This notion implies that the priest is neither divorced from everyday life nor completely submerged in it. It suggests an ideal in which priests are immersed in the life of the faith community but are still able to stand back and articulate the deepest concerns and hopes of the members; an ideal in which priests share the common human condition but are also able to serve wholeheartedly the needs of the community; an ideal in which priests obviously know limitations and sinfulness but must preach mercy and forgiveness. Such priests would not seek unique status and special privilege, but would earn respect as persons serious about following Jesus Christ. In short, the ideal of "inclusive uniqueness" calls upon priests to be such active participants in the human adventure that they effectively illumine and guide the common search for truth and goodness.

There are obvious dangers in this approach. We do not want to create a new version of the clerical caste system or to place even greater pressure on priests to achieve impossible ideals. Nevertheless, as we take up the challenge of creating a new model of priesthood, we must take into account the growing desire of many persons for priests who are, at the same time, both members and leaders of the community.

3. Ministry: Sign of Hope, Source of Nourishment

Ministry is flourishing in the Catholic community. It is difficult to think of a time in history when we have had so many well-prepared people actively engaged in serving the Church and the world. Emphasis on the numerical decline in vocations to the priesthood and the religious life can sometimes obscure this significant development. The Second Vatican Council called for all baptized persons to contribute to the building up of the Body of Christ. We are now witnessing a genuine and widespread response to that call.

Some commentators attribute the decline in priestly vocations to hedonism in the culture and indifference in the Church. This analysis neglects the obvious impact of mandatory celibacy. But it also misses the tremendous countercultural witness offered by a growing number of Church members who serve the Church and the world with great generosity.

Many examples come to mind: The liturgy in most parishes is enhanced by individuals who serve as planners, lectors, musicians, artists and distributors. Candidates for the permanent diaconate are plentiful. In the midst of numerical decline, religious orders have found ways to improve and diversify their ministries. On our campuses, an increasing number of students are being trained to serve the needs of other collegians as "peer ministers." Some large parishes have so much ministerial activity that the pastor cannot even keep up with it—let alone try to control it. In our university parish, we identified 50 people serving in positions of leadership and responsibility. Among priests, I detect a growing interest in improving their pastoral skills. Dedicated parishioners attend workshops to develop their ministerial talents and meet regularly with peers for support.

Thus, in the midst of all the well-publicized problems in the Church as a whole, we have a genuine and powerful sign of hope evident at the local level. Ministry of all types is flourishing as never before.

With this increase of highly-motivated ministers, the problem of fatigue and burnout is also intensified. Full-time ministers tend to get swallowed up in never-ending demands; those who serve part-time are hard-pressed to balance responsibilities to their jobs and to Church activities. Ministers often get to the point where they feel spiritually drained with nothing more to give.

When burnout threatens, we need to find nourishment in the very service we perform. We must learn to *receive* new strength, inspiration and motivation from our ministerial life, rather than always thinking of ministry in terms of giving to others.

Contemporary theology helps us to achieve this important shift in perspective and attitude by offering the following framework: All human beings are called by name and held in Gracious Hands. We walk a common path supported by a Source beyond our control and lured by a Goal which promises fulfillment. Life can be trusted because the Mystery enveloping us desires and works for our happiness and wholeness. For believers, life is filled with clues to the Divine Presence, ranging from the insistent call of conscience to the simple warmth of a smile. For us Christians, this divine love and truth is most clearly manifested in Jesus of Nazareth, who has definitively brought salvation to the world. We celebrate his victory over the dark forces by gathering for the Eucharist, which is a sign of the solidarity of the whole human family.

Within this theological framework, ministry can never simply be the type of giving which drains and frustrates. Since the people we serve are already touched by grace and aware of revelation, we can expect to receive from them both insight and inspiration concerning the things of God. In performing the works of mercy, we can find renewed personal motivation from individuals who carry the cross with grace. We simply need to allow people to minister to us by remaining open to their pain as well as to their experience of God's strengthening grace.

Those dedicated to the often frustrating work of peace and justice can find comfort in a God who never abandons his people. The kingdom of justice and peace is a gift from God whose persuasive power will ultimately prevail. This faith perspective allows ministers to work with hope, if not optimism. We need not carry the fatiguing burden of ultimate frustration, for no energy expended for peace and justice is ever wasted. Furthermore, oppressed persons are not mere recipients of sympathy from the fortunate. They are, rather, companions and partners on the common journey with their own wisdom and energy to contribute. Hearing the cries of the poor can therefore mean receiving as well as giving.

The ministry of teaching and formation can also be a source of spiritual energy. Teachers and students engaged in a common quest for wisdom often find that their roles are reversed as the instructors become the learners. Those dedicated to teaching and formation are thus motivated to deepen and extend their knowledge. Genuine dialogue is a fitting way to search for truth in a world shaped by a universal revelation accessible to all. Ministers who facilitate the intellectual and spiritual growth of even just a few persons often experience a deep joy grounded in the power of the Spirit who makes the whole process of formation possible.

This same general approach can be applied to all forms of ministry. Compassionate presence to persons in need can produce a two-way energy flow if we remain open to the unique strengths of others, as well as to their needs and weaknesses.

Ministry properly involves sacrifice, dedication and self-giving. But when we are genuinely open to others and responsive to the ever-present Spirit, ministry can also generate renewed energy and greater self-actualization. Prayer and meditation, which are absolutely necessary for renewing our inner life, also have an inherent power to attune us to the Source of energy available in the very process of serving others.

4. RCIA: A New Perspective on Sacraments

I hear a lot of positive feedback from people who have recently joined the Catholic community by going through the RCIA—the Rite of Christian Initiation for Adults. This extended process of prayer, study, group interaction and liturgical initiation is designed to immerse individuals gradually into the life of the faith community. Comments by persons who have gone through the process point to the strengths of the program:

- "I wanted to do it quickly and simply, but I am really glad I went through the longer and more formal procedure."

- "The support of the other catechumens was really important—we all learned from each other."

- "It was a time of real spiritual growth for all of us."

- "I think the process deepened the quality of the decision we all made: It has for me the same kind of seriousness as the decision about marriage."

- "The preparation made the Easter Vigil so much more meaningful; the personal approach enabled the ceremony to really touch my heart."

- "I'm personally very grateful to the staff and people in the parish who were so friendly and made me feel as though I really belong to this community."

- "My sponsor told me she found a great deal of inspiration in observing the dedication of the catechumens in our group."

- "I came to appreciate the time of further instruction after Easter because it gave me a better understanding of the faith."

Surely not everyone is so enthusiastic about their catechumenate experience. But this renewed process is clearly an improvement over past procedures and appears to be working well in many parishes.

Liturgists have been claiming that the RCIA will prove to be one of the most significant reforms of the post-Vatican II era. They believe that this whole process by which adults are gradually initiated into the Catholic community will help renew all aspects of parish life and transform parishes into more attractive and welcoming communities. Veteran Church members will be forcefully reminded of the need for adult commitment to the faith as they observe other adults inquiring about the Church, going through a long period of formation, publicly declaring their decision at the Rite of Election during Mass and continuing their instruction afterwards. The RCIA is thus viewed as a catalyst for growth for all parishioners.

It would seem wise to keep such expectations in perspective as ideals collide with reality. We already see a tendency to apply the new approach rigidly, forgetting the need to adapt it to local conditions. The introduction of mysterious terms—such as *catechumen, rite of election, scrutiny* and, especially, *mystagogy*—does not assure that a genuine sense of mystery will pervade our parishes. Some people will still enter the Catholic community simply as a mater of convenience. Others will find that the conversion aspect of RCIA does not really apply to them because their real goal is to find a more congenial place to live out the Christian faith they have already accepted.

Local parishes will continue to be a mixture of grace and sin, despite a vastly improved approach to initiating new members. In short, there are no panaceas for Church reform. We need only recall our high hopes for the vernacular liturgy, for parish councils and for a Mass celebrated facing the people.

To make the most of the genuine potential of the RCIA, we must match the new approaches with improved attitudes. Contemporary theology offers important perspectives and insights which can help us tap the great potential of the RCIA without falling into utopian idealism or doctrinaire rigidity.

Invitation, Not Magic

Sacraments are not magical rites by which we plug into an automatic and exclusive pipeline to an infinite treasury of grace. They are, rather, invitations to respond freely to God's offer of a share in the divine life. They are symbolic actions which cause grace precisely by signifying it. In other words, the very celebration of the rite has the power to open our minds and hearts, making us more receptive to God's love which always surrounds us, waiting for a response. Grace is increased and our personal relationship to God is deepened in proportion to our responsiveness to God's initiative—not by some automatic mechanism.

Grace is always and everywhere operative in our world. Sacraments are the *visibility* of this grace. Far from being exclusive channels of God's love, sacraments are numerically the extraordinary means of sharing in the divine life. Most people in the history of the world have been reborn, strengthened, nourished, healed, forgiven and directed by God apart from participation in the sacraments.

God's gracious activity on our behalf is not limited to liturgical encounters but is found in and through all of life. Sacraments are good for us because they remind us of what God is doing always and everywhere. They are helpful because they fit our nature as bodily, social, historical creatures who need visible reminders, community celebrations and periodic high points to focus our relationship with the Mystery surrounding us. The RCIA, by its very nature as adult instruction, assumes that sacramental activity involves free response, openness of heart and inspirational ritual.

Community Event, Not Private Ceremony

Sacraments are not private ceremonies which communicate grace to privileged individuals. They are community celebrations—official acts of an assembly of Christians. The sacraments are the way the Church officially actualizes itself, makes itself visible and carries on its mission of being an effective sign of the Risen Lord. Sacraments happen when the Church exercises its fundamental function of being a community of grace for individuals at decisive moments in their lives.

The RCIA helps restore this traditional notion of the sacraments. The RCIA insists on the role of the community in the process and celebrates the official initiation at the Easter Vigil—the most important liturgical activity of the year.

Process, Not Isolated Moment

Sacraments are part of a lifelong process of putting on the mind of Christ—not single momentary encounters with Christ, unconnected with past and future. They are high points in the human adventure, which always involve us in a relationship with the Lord of history. They are privileged moments when we are attuned to the special touch of the One who is always life-giving Spirit for us.

We bring our ambivalent past and our immediate preparation to the sacramental meeting with the Risen Lord. We take away light for the dark days in the valley and strength for the draining struggles of the long haul. The RCIA highlights this process with its long period of preparation, its integral celebration of Baptism, Confirmation and First Eucharist at the Easter Vigil, and its subsequent time of further instruction and integration into the community. Here the sacramental activity is clearly seen as a high point which focuses on the past and illumines the future.

An Adult Model for Baptism

From the perspective provided by the RCIA, Baptism cannot be thought of simply as a means of snatching a soul stained by original sin from the threat of eternal damnation. Rather, Baptism is an initiation into a community, where the divine love which sustains all people from the first moments of existence is properly named and fittingly celebrated. The adult catechumen shares in God's grace long before the waters of Baptism are poured. This forces a rethinking of our notion of original sin and our understanding of infant Baptism. We must move beyond the Augustinian position which views the unbaptized as dominated by the taint of original sin and subject to eternal damnation.

Original sin is, indeed, the universal and permanent flaw found in people and society; it has codetermined human existence ever since the sin of the first humans. But it seems more consonant with the theology of the RCIA to recognize that this "sin of the world" has always coexisted with a more powerful grace and has always been encompassed by God's love. In other words, there has never been a time in history when human beings were totally under the sway of sin and when grace was completely absent.

This suggests that when a baby is conceived, it is immediately surrounded by divine love and is already a member of God's family. If a baby dies before being baptized, there is no need to fear damnation nor to resort to the fanciful theory of limbo. We can confidently trust in the triumph of God's love which brings about the salvation of the infant. And when infant Baptism is celebrated, we should emphasize the role of the parents and the gathered assembly, who are called upon to make a conscious response to God who always takes the initiative in offering greater participation in the divine life. In addition, we realize that this baby, who is made a member of a specific Christian group through Baptism, is entering upon a process which will call for a developing personal appropriation of the faith and, eventually, an adult commitment to Christ.

The RCIA makes it clear that the adult model of Baptism is the norm for understanding what the sacrament is all about.

5. Participation: The Means, Not the End, of Liturgy

At the Second Vatican Council, the bishops issued this important directive: "In the restoration and promotion of the sacred liturgy, this full and active participation by all the people is to be considered before all else" (*Constitution on the Sacred Liturgy*). Large numbers of Catholics in the United States have taken this directive with great seriousness. Liturgists have offered guidance on how to improve participation. Musicians have written new music to entice more people to sing. Parish liturgical committees have designed ways to get more of the congregation involved. Pastors have encouraged their people to participate more fully in the Mass. Parishioners have learned more about the liturgy and have sought more active roles.

This cumulative effort has produced impressive results. In just a few decades, we have moved from clerically-dominated silent Masses to participative liturgies with a variety of ministers playing their proper roles. Statistical studies, moreover, indicate that parishioners in parishes which have initiated the participatory reforms of Vatican II are much more satisfied with the liturgy than are parishioners in parishes which have resisted these reforms.

Despite this progress, however, all is not well. Those who accept the goal of increased participation are often not satisfied with the results. Some parishioners complain that they want to play a more active role at Mass but the pastor is against it. Planners are often disappointed when their innovative liturgies remain spectator events. Liturgical leaders report that participation at Saturday Masses, as well as Sunday evening liturgies, is far below the standards of the main

Masses on Sunday mornings. Pastors get frustrated with the people who sit in the back and don't sing.

Other Catholics are more resistant to the call for greater participation. They voice a variety of complaints. The busy liturgy limits reflection time. Singing at Communion time disrupts the intimacy of the moment. Directions about when to sit and stand, what to sing, and how to pray are annoying. For most of these persons, repeated urgings to participate more in the liturgy simply produce resentment.

These examples suggest a fundamental tension between reform-minded liturgists, pastors and parishioners who have made participation their central aim, as the Council requested, and those who sense that this emphasis on participation is diminishing the quality of their worship. To resolve this conflict we must reexamine the nature and function of liturgy in the Christian life.

Liturgical celebrations both symbolize the continuing salvific activity of God in the world and prepare us to be faithful witnesses and instruments of the reign of God. The real goal of liturgy, therefore, is not participation; it is authentic worship and faithful service. The quality of liturgy should not be judged primarily by how many people sing. The more important indicators are how authentically the celebration reflects the divine presence and how effectively it prepares people to carry on the work of Christ.

Liturgy is indeed a communal action which, by its very nature, calls for participation. But this active involvement is for the sake of worship and formation, not an end in itself. Thus the purpose of liturgy planning is to determine the kind and amount of participation which will help the congregation praise God and appropriate the gospel—not to maximize participation at any cost.

It is interesting to examine what liturgical leaders mean when they complain about "lack of participation." They usually do not mean that people are failing to go to Communion, listen to the readings, say the common prayers, sign themselves at the appropriate times or assume the correct postures; most people at Mass now do these things. Nor are they upset about the few people who still say the rosary during Mass or refuse to participate in the greeting of peace; these constitute a small and dwindling percentage of the congregation. They probably are somewhat frustrated by those who come late and leave early. But the real source of irritation is that people do not sing.

For many liturgical leaders, singing has become the barometer by which participation is judged. This is unfortunate. For while singing does have great power to bind people together, to express deep feelings and to enhance the ritual action, it should not be the primary norm for judging participation. Other factors, such as listening to the readings, saying the Lord's Prayer and going to Communion, are obviously more important.

Further reflection on the way liturgy functions helps illumine this question of participation. As a type of symbolic ritual, liturgy shapes our consciousness and structures our imagination. Through repeated participation in the familiar rituals, we come to know what it means to be a member of a Church with a specific set of beliefs and practices. For us Christians, the liturgy keeps alive the memory of Jesus and helps us to put on the mind of Christ. Active participation in the Mass prepares us to discern God's compassionate presence in our everyday lives and to work for God's cause in the world. Worshiping regularly with others establishes a sense of solidarity based on shared meanings and values. Simply by gathering for the Eucharist, we support one another and provide motivation and encouragement for the struggle to live out gospel values in our pluralistic, secularized world.

This reflection suggests some principles and guidelines for fostering liturgical participation:

1. Ritual derives much of its power from familiar repetition, which opens up space for prayerful worship. People participate better if they know, in general, what is happening and can follow easily. Surprises may be nice at a party, but not at Mass.

2. Prudent liturgical adaptation takes into account the dominant characteristics and destructive aspects of our pluralistic culture. For example, our noisy, busy world suggests the need for more silence at Mass. Such communal silence can be a calming and enriching form of group participation. It is intriguing that quiet, reflective late Sunday evening Masses are becoming popular on campuses around the country.

3. In our secularized culture, the meaning of our liturgical symbols is not immediately clear to most parishioners. We therefore need education and instruction so that the rituals can speak directly to mind, heart and imagination. The warnings of the liturgists against explaining the symbols at Mass must be taken seriously. Nevertheless, pastoral ministers find that periodic instruction does enhance the power of the liturgy in the long run.

4. Liturgical leaders should recognize the important ways that most people already participate. They come to church and are part of the assembled congregation—a great sign in itself of God's reign. They join in the common prayers, assume the proper prayer postures and share in the sacred meal. In encouraging further participation through singing, leaders should emphasize selections which enhance the ritual action, especially the acclamations during the Eucharistic Prayer. Liturgical leaders should also be understanding of those who cannot sing or who choose not to for a variety of reasons.

5. Additional practices such as mimed readings, dialogue homilies, elaborate offertory processions, holdings hands during the Our Father and liturgical dance should be included only if they actually further the essential goals of the liturgy.

6. The Notre Dame study (see *The Emerging Parish* by Joseph Gremillion and Jim Castelli, pp. 142-143) suggests certain concrete steps to improve participation: good planning by liturgical leaders; short rehearsal of new music before Mass; a personal greeting by the presider at the beginning; homilies

which apply the readings to daily life; music which fits the ritual action and balances congregational and solo singing; and a social gathering after Mass.

7. Healthy attitudes are more important than particular strategies. We are all coresponsible for the liturgy. We therefore need to come to Mass ready not just to receive and be entertained but to contribute to making the celebration prayerful and formative.

6. Liturgy: Cultivating a Sense of Mystery

The liturgical reforms inaugurated by the Second Vatican Council have generally been welcomed by Catholics who are active in their parishes. An extensive national survey of registered Catholics reports, for example, that 67 percent are happy that hymns are sung at Mass while only four percent wish they were omitted; 27 percent say they don't mind. We see the same positive reaction to other changes: the greeting of peace (61 percent are happy with it to only 12 percent against); Communion in the hand (59 percent to 10 percent); lay readers (60 percent to six percent). Even the least popular changes, communion from the cup and women distributors, still have over twice as many positive supporters as opponents who wish they were omitted. (See the report on the Notre Dame study in *The Emerging Parish* by Joseph Gremillion and Jim Castelli.)

Despite this generally positive statistical picture, we still hear many complaints about the way the Eucharist is celebrated. One of the most common is that the liturgical reforms have robbed the Eucharist of the sense of mystery which was so evident in the traditional Mass. A social activist sister misses the Gregorian chant and finds that high-energy progressive liturgies fail to satisfy her longing for repose. A widower notes that he misses the bells at the consecration and kneeling for Communion because these gave him a sense that something very holy was happening at

Mass. A university professor insists that the more rational and intelligible the Mass is, the less it touches her imagination and lifts her spirit. A corporate executive resents the efforts of priests to get him to sing because it distracts him from worshiping almighty God. A thoughtful lawyer complains that the contemporary liturgy is bland; it diminishes the awesome sense of God's transcendence and thus reduces the impact of experiencing God's immanence in Communion. A collegian reports that she does not like holding hands or dialogue homilies because they make Mass seem like just another social event.

These complaints about the loss of a sense of mystery prompt a reexamination of the very nature and function of liturgy. Along with its important formative power, liturgy enables us to recognize and celebrate God's saving activity in the world on our behalf. Thus a correct understanding of the liturgy is rooted in an accurate analysis of the divine-human relationship which it symbolizes.

The Bible portrays God as the One who calls all people to a faithful and generous response to the divine initiative. This God is *both* the transcendent, all-holy Lord who judges the world *and* the immanent loving Spirit who sustains and energizes the human adventure. We humans are *both* knowers who can recognize the presence of the Lord *and* lovers who can respond to the divine call. God's saving work has *both* a communal dimension *and* an individual aspect. The Lord saves us as a member of a holy people but always calls each of us by name. The divine cause is already being accomplished on this earth but will be complete only at the end of time. Although human life is encompassed and guided by divine grace, sin continues to stalk and threaten us. Our confidence in the ultimate triumph of grace is grounded in Jesus Christ, the final prophet who irrevocably joins the divine and the human. His death and resurrection has made definitive God's promise to save us.

Authentic liturgy must respect the dialogic character of our relationship to God and the tensions built into it. At Mass God speaks and we respond, just as we are supposed to do in everyday life. The liturgy of the Word, which recalls

God's saving deeds in history, leads into the action of the Eucharist, which is our opportunity to join Christ in offering thanks to the Father. The Mass should also respect and illumine the tensions built into the human condition between grace and sin, death and resurrection, creature and creator and the individual and the community.

An upbeat Mass which effectively excludes the persons struggling with the limitations of sin and death would be as off the mark as a deadening liturgy which provides no sense of the final triumph of grace. Likewise, planners and presiders who force a false sense of community on an unwilling congregation fail to respect the inevitable tension between individuals and the community. Styles of liturgical celebration which tend to reduce the inexhaustible mystery of God to a kindly, predictable grandfather betray the tension between transcendence and immanence and undercut our proper sense of creaturehood.

Although Vatican II described the liturgy as the "summit" of Christian life, it seems more accurate and helpful to give the highest place to the life of charity lived in the real world. The most important thing for us is to respond to the call of God by living out the law of love. Salvation is tied, primarily, to a life of service and not to attending Mass. Liturgy is symbolic action which celebrates God's initiative and our responses in our daily experiences. The key to recovering the sense of mystery in the liturgy is therefore to become more aware of the ways the Gracious Mystery is at work in our everyday lives and to find a liturgical style which illumines and focuses these experiences.

There is no doubt that the Tridentine liturgy with its Gregorian chant and Latin language, bells and incense, Communion rails and detailed rubrics had an inherent power to create a sense of mystery. This pre-Vatican II liturgical style was dominated by images of height suggested by the gestures of the priest, the uplifting character of the Gregorian chant and the upward thrust of the Gothic architecture. These images worked well because Catholics experienced God in their everyday lives as transcendent, as the Lord above who guides and judges.

For many contemporary people, however, the dominant metaphor for describing the experience of God in their lives is not height but depth. God is the immanent source which nourishes our being, the sustaining ground which supports all our activities, the inner light which illumines our minds, the interior Spirit which inspires our hearts. We look for God not "up in the sky" but by probing everyday experience in greater depth.

Our liturgical changes reflect this switch in the dominant metaphor which pervades modern culture. Our task is to celebrate the liturgy in such a way that it illumines and evokes the immanent sense of mystery which we already experience in our life in the world. When the assembly gathers for Mass in a warm and friendly way on the basis of equality, it symbolizes the best of our experiences—the times we live and act on the basis of mutuality and love rather than domination and coercion. When the dialogic interplay between the liturgy of the Word and the liturgy of the Eucharist is made clear in word and gesture, it reminds us of the God who calls us by name in the midst of our daily activities.

If lectors proclaim the readings with meaning and homilists suggest helpful applications, the liturgy of the Word has a surprising power to reinforce the good we are already doing and to move us to more effective action on behalf of the kingdom. If the Eucharistic Prayer is said thoughtfully and prayerfully, it can express our abiding gratitude to the God who always loves and sustains us. When the greeting of peace is an authentic symbolic action, it can express our conviction that the transcendent God is manifested in all the people we encounter. When receiving Communion is prayerful, it can focus all the times we have known the intimate presence of the Lord in both private moments and group settings.

Our contemporary liturgy need not be bland or busy. As a symbolic celebration of the death and resurrection of Christ, it maintains its inner power to illumine the tensions of life and to evoke a sense of mystery. Our challenge is to combine careful planning and reverent celebration, verbal participation and communal silence so that the liturgical celebration resonates with our daily efforts to find the infinite in the finite and the extraordinary in the ordinary. Liturgy is an opportunity to name and celebrate the Gracious Mystery which sustains and guides our lives.

7. Wedding Celebrations: Moments of Grace

Everything about the ceremony contributed to the dreamlike character of the event: the colorful stained-glass window depicting the Assumption of Mary, the attractive royal blue dresses of the attendants, the familiar wedding songs and hymns. The bride and groom brought an especially lofty idealism to the occasion, as well as deep hopes for a happy married life together.

My role as celebrant of the wedding Mass took on added significance since the groom was my oldest nephew. I felt especially proud of David, a good and sensitive young man, who has always evoked a special fondness in my heart. Hours of conversation with him and his devoted fiancée, Michele, gave me some feeling for the common dream which brought them to the point of publicly pledging lifelong commitment to one another.

Their choice of readings for the wedding Mass and the commentaries they wrote on them for my benefit gave shape and content to this common dream. I tried to articulate their vision in my homily, confident that it would have a more universal message for those gathered to celebrate the awesome event of two people making mutual vows of fidelity before God and placing many of their hopes for happiness in the hands of another human being.

My comments on Romans (12:1-18) related Paul's powerful statements on the ideals of the Christian life to the dreams of the bride and groom. "Do not let your love be a pretense" suggests a vision of married life based on genuine caring. "Do not model yourselves on the behavior of the world" indicates that the real pattern for Christian marriage is not found in the individualism and consumerism fostered by our culture but in the generous sacrificial love exemplified by Jesus Christ. "Have a profound respect for each other" forms the basis for a true partnership in which both spouses overcome their desires to control and concentrate instead on encouraging the beloved to develop as a unique individual. "Treat everyone with equal kindness" and "Live at peace with everyone" encourages married couples to allow the love they share to flow over into service to the world and care for the less fortunate. "If you have hope, this will make you cheerful" validates the dream of lovers that a life together based on mutual giving and receiving and firmly grounded in trust in the power of God can bring a deep and abiding sense of joy and satisfaction.

The couple told me they wanted to place this passage from Romans on the wall of their apartment. I hoped they would write it upon their hearts as well. It contains not only high ideals but also practical wisdom for married life.

At weddings I often have the urge to call on married couples in the congregation to stand up and give honest expression to the trials, crosses, difficulties, temptations and failures they have experienced in their lives together. Resisting this urge, I tried to summarize some of the common problems I have heard expressed over many years of marriage counseling:

- He won't share his feelings with me.

- She does not respect me or the work I do.

- My spouse is always around and I have no space for myself.

- We fight over how to spend the money.

- We seem to have fallen out of love.

- It is hard to keep showing the little signs of endearment which used to flow so easily.

- The infidelities and lies have destroyed my trust.

- I get tired of dealing with my partner's main faults.

- We are so busy we don't have time for one another.

- Our sex lives move between routine and nonexistent.

- We have trouble meshing two careers.

- Our disagreements on how to raise children are a continuing source of tension.

Marriage is an extremely difficult relationship to make work. The problems are multiplied by trends in contemporary culture such as frequent divorce, dual careers, busy lifestyles, stressful jobs, unreal expectations and the prevalence of drugs. The beautiful dream shared by David and Michele will inevitably encounter the harsh realities of life. Their idealism will be assailed by the same kind of dark forces which attack all modern marriages.

Marriage vows demand a resolute effort to avoid cynicism and indifference. The challenge is to face the problems and to mobilize love and intelligence in moving toward solutions. The eyes of faith, however, discern hidden resources in this struggle.

In John's Gospel (15:12-16), Jesus says he calls us not servants but friends because he has revealed to us the wisdom learned from the Father. He has given us the command to love one another as he has loved us. He has commissioned us to go forth and to produce fruits which have an enduring significance. Christ walks the path with married couples, sustaining and enriching their love. It is the power of his Spirit which provides daily energy and surprising resources for avoiding cynicism and keeping the marital dream alive. My prayer for my nephew and his bride included the hope that they would use the inevitable clash between their ideals and reality as a means of deepening their love.

I then invited the married couples present to activate their imaginations by remembering their own wedding day and recalling the visions, hopes and ideals which brought them to that moment. I suggested that today's beautiful wedding could be a catalyst for reactivating their own dream and for making a new effort to embody it in their daily lives.

No matter what their ages or how long they have been married, couples can use the occasion of a wedding to renew their commitments to live in mutual and lasting fidelity. Guided by their original vision, they can work together to improve their communication and to heal the wounds inflicted on each other. Recalling some of their better encounters, they can search for ways to bring back some of the zest and chemistry to their relationship. Spouses can try again to get rid of a fault or habit which hurts their partner. Dialogue can be initiated on some of the continuing areas of disagreement and conflict. Couples can resolve that they will not settle for mediocrity in their marriage. Remembering the religious character of their wedding, couples can make a more vigorous effort to grow together spiritually and to make Christ a more intimate part of their common journey. By allowing their original dreams to stir their imaginations, all the couples present can find ways to solidify their relationships and deepen their love.

Experience tells me that many married couples do have their imaginative processes stimulated by the remarkable power of weddings. Some couples do seize the moment to come up with constructive actions. Comments after my nephew's wedding solidified this conviction:

- "My wife poked me in the ribs when you talked about recapturing the chemistry."

- "The whole ceremony provoked some genuine soul-searching on my part."

- "You got us thinking."

- "I got teary and then realized I was reliving my own wedding."

- "You get so busy that you forget about the dreams you had in those first years."

- "We talked after the ceremony and decided to work on improving our communications."

- "Thanks for speaking to us as well as to the bride and groom."

- "I am glad you brought in the realism—it has been a struggle for us."

- "My husband said he feels like renewing our vows."

- "We have never prayed together much; maybe we should do more of that. It might help."

The efforts of my nephew and his bride to arrange a beautiful and meaningful ceremony had produced an unintended by-product. It provided everyone present, especially the married couples, with an opportunity to reflect more deeply on their own relationships in the light of the Scripture passages.

In the prayers of petition, I then invited the assembly of family and friends to pray that the presence of the Lord who calls us friends would be very real to the newly-married couple. Together we prayed that they would find the wisdom and courage, especially in the difficult times, to maintain their idealism and to live out their dream.

Attending weddings, or even reflecting on them from a distance, can be a great catalyst for prayerful meditation and spiritual growth. It can help both individuals and couples live out their dreams.

Chapter Four

Promoting Ecumenical and Interfaith Dialogue

1. Fundamentalists: Why Conversation Breaks Down

After everyone else had departed from my contemporary theology class, a young man remained seated, poring over his large Bible. "I hardly know where to begin," he said. He then went on to outline his objections to the method of modern biblical criticism I had employed in my treatment of Jesus Christ as portrayed in the Gospels.

Speaking thoughtfully, he pointed out that everything in the Bible must be taken literally. If one admitted the slightest error in the Scriptures, the whole thing would collapse. The historical method I had used in class was totally wrong, he insisted, because it says in the Bible that all Scripture is inspired by God and is useful for reproving and teaching—teaching the truth, he quickly added.

Then a strange thing happened. He looked at me and said, "What do you think of that?" The attack had ceased and, contrary to all my expectations based on previous experiences with biblical fundamentalists, he really appeared to be interested in my response. I asked him, in a gentler tone than I usually manage in such situations, how he handled certain apparent contradictions and discrepancies in the Bible, such as the creation of light before the sun in Genesis.

"There was an alternate source which accounted for the light before the sun was created," he said, giving the typical answer based on a fundamentalist commentary he had recently read. He went on to speak passionately against evolutionary theory, revealing in the process that he was a graduate student with a minor in geology. Surprised, I asked if it bothered him to be out of step with the general thinking of the scientific community. He answered decisively, "No, it is more important to me to be faithful to the Bible and to judge the scientific facts from the viewpoint of the creation account in Genesis."

The conversation turned to salvation. He revealed to me, with sadness in his voice, that he had great doubts about whether his own father was saved. In fact, he was forced to believe that most people have not been saved because they have never explicitly accepted Jesus Christ. I asked how he reconciled this with the biblical image of a loving God. He said, a bit unconvincingly, that it didn't bother him and that he still believed God was loving.

I felt compassion for this young man who seemed to be experiencing a good deal of psychic discomfort beneath his calm statements. I told him that I respected his sincerity. I also said that I understood the way his scriptural interpretation provided him with a comprehensive vision of life and a practical guide for living as a Christian. I asked him if he could accord my position the same respect. He replied with what I took to be sadness: "No, I cannot allow that. I can't compromise and leave any cracks in my position." He added that he could see how that might hurt me and make genuine dialogue impossible. But he had to remain faithful to the Bible at all costs, for it contained God's truth.

We shook hands and, as he departed, I told him how enjoyable it was to talk calmly and reasonably with a biblical fundamentalist. I said I hoped we could converse again.

But my intuition told me that we wouldn't, and my head told me why: Such conversation was simply too threatening to this bright, well-read, obviously sensitive and apparently confident young man.

Our conversation had moved to the level of conflicting worldviews instead of remaining focused on the more comfortable area of interpreting individual Bible verses. The young man was moved to examine his fundamental assumptions more carefully and to recognize some of the questionable consequences of his position. When he found himself confronted by the challenge of a very different interpretive scheme, he instinctively knew that he had to reject it immediately and totally. He could not allow genuine dialogue nor accord my position any measure of respect because he correctly understood that any crack or compromise would endanger the whole of his system.

George Marsden's scholarly and balanced *Fundamentalism and American Culture* offers a great deal of help in understanding this young man. It provides background and context for recognizing fundamentalism as a comprehensive system.

Approximately five million Americans call themselves fundamentalists. Their position was originally formulated as a response to religious and cultural factors found in a distinctive combination in the United States.

The dominant Calvinist tradition, with its moralistic tendencies and its emphasis on "Scripture alone," provides a matrix for the fundamentalist contention that the whole of God's truth is found in the Bible. We Catholics, who have a much stronger sense of the living tradition of the Church, may have trouble understanding the temptation to make the scriptural text into an absolute. We probably can get the best feel for the way Scripture functions for fundamentalists by recalling the way papal infallibility works for traditionalist Catholics. It is the glue which holds the whole system together—and any attack upon it threatens one's whole way of life.

The "Scripture alone" theme came to the fundamentalists filtered through the American revivalist movement. It consciously presented the biblical message in simple opposites of good and evil, truth and falsehood. Imagine a traditional tent meeting with an emotional preacher who graphically portrays the threat of Satan and his evil activities in the world. He then recalls the great promise of salvation to those who accept the Lord Jesus into their hearts. The student in my class presented his worldview in just that way—a gigantic battle between Satan and Christ in which our major weapon is the inspired, inerrant Word of God in the Bible.

Scottish common-sense philosophy also shaped American fundamentalism. This philosophy, which is reflected in the thought of our founding fathers, stressed the ability of the human mind to comprehend reality in a direct and straightforward way. Fundamentalists have clearly picked up this positive assessment of human reason and use it to show that true science, common sense and the Bible are never in contradiction. Each, in its own way, reveals the truth of God's Word.

Fundamentalists have never been fideists who celebrate biblical faith and deny reason. On the contrary, they use science and reason to corroborate biblical teaching. Thus the fundamentalist geology student told me that science has shown that a universal flood was possible, and that would account for the fossil remains discovered by paleontologists. He claims to reject only "bad" science—for example, the kind of hypothesis which Darwin and the evolutionists have forced on people in violation of common sense.

In the 20th century, this combination of revivalist evangelical Christianity and hard-headed common-sense philosophy encountered the expanding influence of modern biblical criticism and the general acceptance of evolutionary theory. The result was the modern phenomenon known as fundamentalism. It attracted individuals who felt isolated from the mainstream of American life.

These fundamentalists, in reaction to mainstream culture, formulated a comprehensive worldview based on the inerrancy of Scripture. People were neatly divided into those who lived in the supernatural light created by total acceptance of God's Word and those who lived in the natural darkness of unbelief. In addition, a growing sense of isolation produced a renewed effort to identify this religious position with the traditional American way of life. This was coupled with an aggressive evangelization program to convert more people to their way of thinking.

This analysis sheds light on the aggressive political tactics of some right-wing Christians. They are not a strange aberration but an intensified and contemporary manifestation of tendencies built into a movement which felt itself estranged from the dominant political and religious life of the country.

The graduate student in my class feels alienated from the dominant thinking of the academic world. Fundamentalism offers him a comprehensive and coherent system for interpreting reality based ultimately on a literal reading of an error-free Bible. From this perspective, he had to view me and the contemporary theology I represented as the enemy. His natural response was to protect himself against this radical challenge to the religious viewpoint which provides him security and comfort.

A sense of the historical development and distinctive features of fundamentalism can help us understand the polarized approach often adopted by its adherents. It should also give us greater compassion for these Christians whose fragile belief system simply cannot tolerate genuine dialogue.

2. The "Born-Again": A Framework for Honest Discussion

According to recent polls, there are an estimated 30 to 50 million persons in the United States who consider themselves "born-again Christians." This is a staggering statistic. Even in the absence of a more precise breakdown of the data, it invites examination and comment.

Who would answer yes to the question, "Are you born again?"

The largest group consists of Protestant evangelicals who grew up with this explicit language as part of their religious heritage. Adults who have accepted Jesus Christ as their personal savior often find this terminology congenial. An estimated five million fundamentalists have their roots in the privatizing wing of Evangelical Protestantism, and they point to "spiritual rebirth" as the ground for their acceptance of the inerrancy of the Scriptures. For those Christians who expect the imminent return of Christ, being "born again" is what assures them a place among the 144,000 who will enjoy the "rapture."

Many of those Catholics who find their spiritual home in the Charismatic movement would also likely answer yes to the "born again" question. They speak about their deeper religious experiences in terms of a rebirth which brings the gifts of the Spirit. They often find kinship with Protestant friends who come out of the Pentecostal and Holiness movements and who speak of being reborn through the "baptism of the Spirit."

No doubt some more traditional Catholics would also answer yes because they understand the sacrament of Baptism as a new birth into the life of the Church. Their response, however, bears a distinctive meaning quite different from the affirmations of evangelicals.

Who, then, would answer no?

Likely candidates include those who are uncomfortable with the born-again language. Some have heard aggressive evangelizers who use such language to produce guilt feelings. Others have encountered groups of born-again Christians who make offensive claims about having a monopoly on God's truth and grace. Still others simply find the talk of spiritual rebirth to be overblown, exaggerated and too emotional.

Political liberals and moderates often associate the born-again theme with extreme right-wing politics which they find intolerant and divisive. And many people today respond negatively to the TV evangelists who use born-again language as part of energetic campaigns to raise money.

Then there are those who respond negatively to this question of rebirth because they experience their lives more in terms of continuity than discontinuity. They cannot point to a dramatic conversion experience or a single life-changing decision. For such people, Christian life is more a matter of organic growth and steady progress. They simply do not understand or appreciate born-again language because it does not reflect their own religious development.

How can dialogue between the born again and other Christians be facilitated? One place to begin is with an understanding of human existence which sees life as a mix of continuity and discontinuity.

We are historical creatures called to move toward greater integration, freedom and fulfillment—without ever being able to achieve completely these human goals during our lifetimes. In this process, however, we all experience key moments when the call is clearer and our response is fuller. Each person's life is punctuated by decisive moments in the midst of the routine and ordinary.

Within this common frame of reference, some experience clear high points and decisive changes, while others find themselves in a gradual process with a great sense of continuity. Neither group, however, finds the experience of the other totally foreign. We all know both continuity and change. This common experience can form the basis for honest dialogue between the born again, who emphasize decisive change, and those Christians who experience a more gradual development.

Several specific cautions can also help facilitate the discussion. Some are directed at those Christians who do not resonate easily with born-again language; others are for Christians that do.

Those who distrust born-again language need to be reminded of the legitimacy of conversion experiences. Through the power of God, individuals do turn their lives around. They can experience a decisive transformation which puts them in tune with the source of their existence. This often brings an exhilarating sense of liberation, a new focus, deeper insights, renewed energy and increased self-esteem—and a great desire to tell others about it in order to draw them into the experience.

When authentic personal development occurs, we can and must attribute it to the power of the Spirit. The fact that the experience may be poorly explained and erroneously interpreted does not take away from its genuine character. If the religious conversion does not immediately transform the reborn person's emotional, imaginative, intellectual and moral life, this does not invalidate the whole event.

Individuals can be deluded and conversions can be artificially manufactured; thus we need to retain our critical intelligence in assessing religious claims. This does not detract, however, from the central point that God's grace does produce dramatic changes in individuals and that such experiences can enlighten and inspire those who follow a steadier course.

The born again also must make adjustments if a productive dialogue is to take place. They cannot begin with the premise that their type of religious experience is superior. Nor can they enter the discussion with the intention of converting others to their brand of piety. Their language should not make it sound as though they have a direct and unambiguous pipeline to God. It is also important to avoid giving the impression of exclusiveness—as though they have the illuminating truth and everyone else walks in the darkness of falsehood.

Those who have known the dramatic moment of rebirth in the Spirit must remember that it is not a once-for-all event. Rather, it functions as a catalyst for further growth. Perhaps in the retelling of their conversion stories, the born again can find a fresh language that does not sound so patterned and programmed. Effective witnessing to the gospel requires prudence as well as zeal.

I recall a man who spoke simply but effectively about a striking transformation in his life. He began by describing his previous situation in which he sensed something was terribly wrong and experienced constant psychic pain.

Through a process which remained mysterious, he found himself enjoying a new life in which everything was changed, the world looked brighter and he felt like a new man. He experienced it all as a gift and was extremely grateful. Finally he expressed his intention to demonstrate his gratitude by a greater effort to love his family and help others. This story, which reflects a genuine born-again experience, is all the more impressive to me for its simplicity and use of ordinary language.

Genuine dialogue between the once-born and the twice-born is possible only if individuals in each group recognize the limitations of their own perceptions and grant a fundamental validity to the experience of others. If we talk together on that basis, we will all come to a deeper knowledge and appreciation of the inexhaustible One who remains beyond our comprehension and imagining.

3. Variety of Religious Experiences: Challenge to Christian Exclusivism

Carol's story highlights the ongoing need to struggle against the exclusive tendencies of Christian groups who claim a monopoly on God's truth and saving grace. She happily shares this portion of her spiritual journey.

Carol grew up in a large Irish-Catholic family on the East Coast, but rebelled against Catholicism during her years in high school. When she came to college, she decided to give her religion another chance. She got very involved in the Catholic community on campus, which did indeed meet her needs for good liturgy and opportunities to learn and serve.

Near the end of her freshman year, Carol became friends with some students who were very involved in an evangelical group on campus. Although she continued to go to Mass regularly, she found herself more and more drawn to this small group of Christians who met regularly to study the Scriptures and to share their experiences of evangelizing other students. Periodically, Carol picked up anti-Catholic messages from some members of the group, often in not-so-subtle comments about her continuing attendance at Mass. Still, she was attracted by the warm and comforting atmosphere in the group and by the sincerity of the members. The clear and definite message of salvation through a commitment to Christ as personal savior appealed to her. She longed for the born-again experience described by many of the collegians in the fellowship.

As time went on, Carol found herself accepting not only the challenging message of total dedication to Jesus Christ but also the exclusive tendencies which surrounded the message. The group commonly assumed that Catholics and mainline Protestants were not really Christians. Judgments were often made about whether individuals were truly born-again Christians or simply hypocrites who were followers of Christ in name only. The dominant sense of the group was that those who were not born again did not know the true God and would not be saved.

This religious exclusivism, as Carol tells it, gradually took over her consciousness and became her dominant way of seeing the world and assessing other people. She did not feel free to date someone who was not born again. She silently accepted the right of the group to challenge any relationships which violated the norm. She increasingly saw herself aligned with a small number of faithful Christians who experienced the secular world as either irrelevant to true believers or as a positive danger to their faith.

At the Catholic Masses on campus, Carol was hearing a very different message: God, the compassionate lover, wills the salvation of *all* people. Divine grace is available to *all* who open their hearts and follow the dictates of conscience. *All* the world's great religious traditions are vehicles of truth and goodness. The world, though flawed by sin, is filled with God's grace.

This line of thought struck Carol as probably heretical, since her deepest convictions were now shaped by the exclusive messages of her nondenominational fellowship. Elements of the Catholic Mass continued to attract her, however, especially sharing in Communion and the reflective moods sometimes created by the liturgy. Unwilling to give up either her close circle of evangelical friends or her regular participation at Mass, she continued to attend both and lived with the tension of the conflicting messages. Her general approach to people and to the world, however, was dominated by the exclusive outlook.

In this tension-filled state, Carol went on a brief vacation during spring break. One day, after lying in the sun near a lake, she headed back through a wooded area to the cottage where she was staying. Suddenly, she experienced an encompassing presence which took over her spirit and flooded her being. She was immediately aware of the beauty of the woods surrounding her. It was as though God the Father was holding the hand of his beloved daughter and saying, "Look at this wonderful world that I have made for your delight." Her eyes were opened, and she saw the grandeur of the world as if observing it for the first time. The one God, who had created and loved her, was also the creator of the whole material world. She sensed the oneness and the unity of it all.

The whole experience lasted only a few minutes, but it continues to be a permanent part of her consciousness. Sometimes the feeling of an encompassing and friendly presence will spontaneously come over her again—not as intense but still very real.

Even though most things in her life have remained the same, she insists that everything is now different. Despite the evils in the world, she remains very aware of its graced condition. Nature now speaks regularly to her of the Divine Presence. She currently enjoys reading all kinds of literature for its own sake and for its power to illumine the human adventure without worrying, as she had previously, if it was written by a genuine Christian or was faithful to biblical teaching. She also finds herself less judgmental about her roommate's Muslim boyfriend. And she has become acutely aware of exclusive religious language, at times feeling great pain over the conflicts it creates with her born-again friends.

During her regular prayer periods, Carol now spends less time reading her Bible and more time silently enjoying God's presence. She finds herself strongly attracted to contemplative spiritual writers, especially Thomas Merton. His book, *Contemplative Prayer*, puts into words much of what she has been feeling. She now thinks of her prayer life as having taken on a contemplative tenor and understands more about the mystical character of her important religious experience near the lake.

At times Carol experiences doubts about her new awareness, and the old exclusive outlook seems to rise up. At those moments she is tempted to squeeze her great moment of awakening into the narrow confines of Christian exclusivism. When she trusts her experience, however, her more open attitude becomes a judgment upon all narrow sectarian religious views.

The struggle for her soul continues. But Carol knows that, in the long run, she cannot deny her experience of the great God whose love encompasses not only her, but all human beings and the whole of reality.

Carol's story, for me, is a striking reminder that we dare not allow the language of religious experience to be co-opted by exclusive Christians. It is dangerous and destructive for one type of Christian spirituality to masquerade as the only one.

Genuine religious experience encompasses more than a sudden born-again experience. The history of Christian spirituality manifests a great variety of religious experiences and many paths leading to the Gracious God. Great prophets, like Amos and John the Baptist, have known God intimately as the one who judges the sins of the world. Great mystics, like Teresa of Avila and Thomas Merton, have known the encompassing and unifying power of the divine light which illumines the whole of reality. Many ordinary people know that God can be found in everyday life and in simple events. Solid individuals, who have struggled with their crosses, recognize that the Spirit is present in the journey itself and not only in the moment of conversion.

The variety of religious experiences granted to persons throughout history stands as a compelling witness against exclusivism. When we recall that God calls each person by name, it becomes clear that spirituality must be pluralistic. The Spirit which breathes where she wills cannot be confined in the narrow circle of sectarian religion.

Carol's profound and moving mystical-type experience came unbidden—as a pure divine gift. It challenged her restricted views of God's revelation and saving grace. Her story invites us to trust our own religious experience, simple and ordinary as it might be, and to test it against the rich and vast Christian tradition with its diverse paths to God. We must be confident of the unique value of our own encounters with the Lord and not let ourselves be intimidated by enthusiastic accounts of striking conversions.

Carol's story prompts an honest self-examination. Religious exclusivism is not the province of only one group, but rather a continuing temptation for all believers. We are well advised to call on the Gracious Mystery to transform our narrowness and to open our minds and hearts to truth, goodness and beauty wherever it is to be found.

4. The Future of Ecumenism: Signals From the Campus

It is difficult these days to detect many signs of what the great Dominican theologian Yves Congar called "ecumenical passion." The movement toward Christian unity which excited and enlightened many of us in the past now seems to be at a standstill, and the future is filled with uncertainty. An exploration of the ecumenical situation on our campuses, where future leaders are being nourished, reveals a good deal about the current state of the movement as well as possible directions for the future.

From this campus perspective, four major types of students appear especially important to me: "traditional Catholics," "ecumenical Christians," "aggressive fundamentalists" and "open searchers." No individual student fits neatly into any one of these types, but they help focus our attention on general tendencies and broad interpretations of complex realities.

Traditional Catholics

Catholic collegians of the traditional type are firmly rooted in their faith and have little understanding of the Protestant or Orthodox world. They grew up in conservative Catholic homes and attended Catholic schools. They had little direct contact with Protestants before coming to college. Their religious education did not include the study of other religions.

These students feel comfortable in their Catholic world and sense no particular need to expand their religious horizons. Their general, unexamined assumption is that Catholics occupy some kind of privileged place in God's plan. They go to Mass regularly and would never think of going to Communion in a Protestant Church.

Although a small percentage of these traditional students become more rigid in their views during their collegiate career, most grow toward greater openness and toleration. Since their exclusive attitudes result more from unexamined assumptions than from a doctrinaire ideology, the thrust toward tolerance generated by the collegiate experience can penetrate their consciousness.

By meeting Protestants who are good people, they come to understand that Christian values are shared by others. Through academic studies they begin to see their own tradition in a larger historical and societal perspective. By living in an academic community which celebrates civil discourse, they assimilate the notion that dialogue is a valuable tool for dealing with differences. These influences have the cumulative effect of making these students more open toward the Protestant world—even toward the possibility of joint worship and intercommunion. In short, the collegiate experience challenges traditional Catholics to examine their religious heritage as well as the assumptions which surround their faith.

Ecumenical Christians

These collegians have a nonexclusive relationship to the Catholic Church. I call these Catholics "ecumenical Christians" because they remain committed to Christ and gospel values but see themselves as having moved beyond the denominational disputes of the past. They call themselves "Catholics" and are at home in the Catholic community, but they retain a fundamental openness to the Protestant Churches, as well as other religious values. They generally come from more liberal Catholic families and have attended public schools. Contact with Protestants has been a normal part of their growing up.

As collegians, these ecumenical Christians worship regularly with the Catholic community, but would not hesitate to attend a Protestant service instead. The laws against intercommunion seem ridiculous to them, as do the mixed marriage promises. They sometimes bring their Protestant friends to Mass, leaving the choice of going to Communion up to them.

These ecumenical Christians have practically no knowledge of the traditional disputes between Catholics and Protestants—and really don't care. Their solution to the continuing divisions among Christians is simply to forget the past and become united. Some of these students will not hesitate to join another Church if the choice of a marriage partner makes this more convenient or if they do not find a Catholic parish which satisfies their needs.

Aggressive Fundamentalists

On campuses we find small but vocal groups of Christian collegians publicly proclaim in word and action that their particular style of belief and piety based on the Bible is the only way of following Christ. Their exclusive outlook leads them to an aggressive style of proselytizing which try to induce individuals to give up their church membership and join a nondenominational group.

These fundamentalists insist on the inerrancy of the Scriptures and focus on the image of Jesus as personal savior. They are more interested in converting others than in entering into honest dialogue. Their gatherings center on the biblical Word, with large doses of personal witness and warm fellowship. These groups are often very attractive to religiously-inclined Catholic students who are searching for deeper experiences of intimate community.

The aggressive proselytizers share the common conviction that Catholics are not saved because they deny the unique mediatorship of Christ by worshiping Mary, and the normative character of Scripture by holding nonbiblical doctrines such as purgatory. The Catholics who join these groups often repeat these stereotypical charges, even though they do not accord with their own experiences of Catholicism.

Many mainline campus ministers are critical of fundamentalist groups becuase their exclusive attitudes and aggressive tactics hurt students, undermine the ecumenical movement and give religion a bad name.

Open Searchers

Among collegians today there is a growing number of "open searchers." These students come from family situations in which the parents did not foster any particular faith commitments in their children.

When these students encounter other collegians who have a solid faith, they feel deprived in ways they find hard to articulate. This causes them to enter upon a search for a deeper way of living which provides a sense of meaning, belonging and rootedness. They feel justified in this search because their parents—who seldom, if ever, attended church—encouraged them to think for themselves and to develop their own philosophy of life.

These searchers are usually attracted to a particular faith community through the influence of friends. After some initial discomfort, they are able to blend into the new religious group quite easily. Their natural tendency is to accept what feels right to them and to reject those teachings and values which do not accord with their own experiences. They are not interested in the disputes of the past among Christians but simply want a religious commitment which satisfies their needs now.

When they decide to join the Church, they do so as adults making a free choice. The RCIA program serves as an excellent vehicle to meet their needs. I anticipate that the number of open searchers will be increasing in the years ahead and that their eclectic approach to religious matters will have an effect on the ecumenical scene.

Insights from the great German Jesuit theologian Karl Rahner (1904-1984) provide a context to explore further these four types. Rahner's theology of grace sets a broad framework which can guide our general approach to ecumenism.

In order to effect the salvation of all persons (1 Timothy 2:4), God has communicated the Spirit to every human being. This divine self-gift which we call "grace" creates a universal revelation which echoes in the hearts and consciences of all people. When individuals respond positively to this call, they manifest a saving faith.

God's self-giving is effective to the degree that human beings are open to it. Christians believe that the divine self-communication found the perfect respondent in Jesus of Nazareth—a man so receptive that he truly is God in our midst. Thus Jesus is for us the definitive Word, the final prophet, the absolute savior.

This theological framework forms the basis for genuine ecumenical dialogue. It avoids both a doctrinaire exclusivism and a mindless relativism. The aggressive fundamentalists have failed to grasp the universality of God's grace and revelation. They do not understand that saving faith can be implicit and anonymous. They restrict God's saving power by limiting its effectiveness to one brand of Christian piety. We must continue to search for ways to bring these fundamentalist groups into the mainstream of ecumenical dialogue. For many of us this has proven to be a most difficult task. But charity must remain our highest ideal, even when dealing with those who want to exclude us from the ranks of true Christians.

Rahner's theology also reminds us that genuine and lasting unity cannot be attained by watering down beliefs and papering over differences. Belief in Christ as the definitive revelation of God suggests that we will all come closer together by deepening our commitment to the Lord and by being more faithful to his teachings. The gospel witness to Christ remains our norm for making judgments about all truth claims and proposed courses of action.

In an important book authored with Heinrich Fries, *Unity of the Churches—An Actual Possibility*, Rahner argues convincingly that all long-standing disputes between Catholics and mainline Protestants are, in principle, solved or solvable. He therefore sees unity as actually possible in the foreseeable future. What would this union of the churches look like and how does Rahner's scenario illumine the ecumenical situation on campus?

Rahner does not envision a strict uniformity in which denominations are asked to give up their distinctive differences in a "lowest common denominator" approach. Nor does he suggest that the Churches of the Reformation return to the Catholic Mother Church, like prodigal sons. On the contrary, Rahner speaks of a "reconciled diversity" or a "conciliar fellowship."

According to this vision, the main Christian denominations would come together in a federation under the servant leadership of the Bishop of Rome, who would be the spokesperson for the gospel ideals which bind all together. The individual Churches would retain their distinctive customs and structures for decision-making, and the Petrine minister would represent the consensus of the partner Churches. All the participating Churches would affirm the common apostolic faith as expressed in the Scriptures and common creeds, especially the Nicene Creed.

The Churches in this conciliar fellowship would not totally reject out-of-hand a doctrine or practice binding in another Church; nor would a particular Church impose on the others a teaching not clearly attested in Scripture. Thus, for example, Protestants would stay open to the possibility that the Assumption says something significant about salvation for all believers, and Roman Catholics would not impose a strict teaching about birth control.

The partner Churches would interact a great deal, recognize one another's ministries, share freely in each other's worship, and gradually enrich the universal Church with their distinctive histories. Ordinations would be celebrated through prayer and the laying on of hands, with the active participation of official Church leaders from other partner Churches, including the Catholic community. In the course of time, this practice would solve the ideological dispute over the validity of Orders.

The ecumenical Christians on campus would certainly fit quite comfortably into a united Church based on Rahner's notion of a "conciliar fellowship." This vision of Christian fellowship puts into a structural framework the personal sensibilities of these students. They already act as if all the disputed questions are solved. They have intuitively adopted Rahner's position that we cannot demand more consensus and uniformity in the federated Church than already exists within the Catholic Church. Put more positively, they are ready to accept and celebrate the kind of pluralism in the united Church that we currently enjoy in the Catholic community. The ease and comfort of these collegians with diverse liturgical expressions prepare them for the diverse forms of worship in a conciliar fellowship which allows member Churches to maintain their distinctive customs and practices.

Given their religious sensibilities, the ecumenical Christians on our campuses can become important leaders in the movement toward a new Christian federation. To be effective, they will need solid theological training and a deeper understanding of the need for the Petrine ministry, the proper role of doctrines and the unifying power of creeds. Providing this type of theological education is a major challenge for theology departments and campus ministry programs.

Although "ecumenical passion" is no more evident on campuses than elsewhere, we can detect signs of hope which augur well for the future. For example, many traditional Church members develop greater tolerance during their collegiate careers, and thereby are better prepared for fruitful dialogue and cooperation with other Christians in the years ahead. The search for truth, which remains an ideal of the academic community, often exposes the distortions and dangers of religious exclusivism. Faith communities on campus are attracting more open searchers and enabling them to experience the wisdom and power of the Christian tradition. Finally, the ecumenical Christians, when true to their best instincts, are harbingers of a united Christian Church which celebrates commitment to Christ, fidelity to tradition and openness to pluralism.

5. Mikhail Gorbachev: Unleashing Spiritual Energy

Historians will debate the precise role of Mikhail Gorbachev in the demise of the Soviet Union and its movement toward a free-market economy. What is unassailable, however, is that during his tenure the cruel and enduring persecution of religion in the Soviet Union ceased and religious communities began to flourish under a newfound freedom. This accomplishment, along with other achievements in the area of civil rights and political freedom at home and abroad, stamp Gorbachev as one of the great liberators of modern times—no matter what final judgment is rendered on his economic policies.

We can gain a better sense of the magnitude of Gorbachev's accomplishments by recalling the horrendous persecution of religion under the Communist regime. Lenin, by the time of his death in 1924, had unleashed a full-scale persecution of believers, thereby implicitly denying Marx's position that religion would simply wither away in the classless society. Under Stalin, the persecution of religion was intensified. In 1929 the Law on Religious Associations mandated that religious groups had no inherent rights and could operate legally only if registered.

An essential element in the campaign against religion was the confiscation of church buildings. It was common for the Communists to attack churches at night, removing the valuables, breaking up the icons and burning the holy vessels. Churches were often turned into museums or buildings for public use. As Alexander Solzhenitsyn later pointed out, the struggle for freedom in Russia centered on the effort to win back the churches as places of worship.

By the time World War II broke out, there were only a few hundred churches in the Soviet Union still open for worship. With the steady advance of Nazi troops into Soviet territory, however, Stalin was forced to turn to the churches for help. On September 4, 1943, he met with three Orthodox bishops and secured their support for the war effort. In return, he allowed several thousand churches to reopen during the 1940s.

In 1959 Nikita Kruschev, often considered more liberal on domestic policies, instituted a renewed attack on religion. He closed most of the churches that had been reopened under Stalin, decimated the monasteries and left only three theological seminaries open in the whole Soviet Union.

A 1961 law deprived the clergy of any direct control over the functions of the local Church, limiting their activities to the celebration of the liturgy. The Churches were forbidden to engage in any social service activities, such as running orphanages or hospitals, because the state was doing such a fine job of providing for all human needs. Church employees were put into the highest tax brackets, and a substantial portion of Church income had to be contributed to the Soviet Peace Fund. There were obligatory courses on atheism in the schools and universities. Atheistic museums were established in the cities, often housed in former cathedrals. The media frequently attacked religion. Authorities identified churchgoers and often punished them economically.

Despite this long period of persecution, the Soviet regime could not destroy the religious spirit of its people. By the time Gorbachev came to power in 1985, an estimated 80 million Orthodox Christians still existed in the Soviet Union despite the great number of martyrs. Around 60 million Muslims, located primarily in the Central Asian republics, also continued to practice their religion. Approximately 10 million Catholics, heavily concentrated in the Ukraine and Lithuania, were clinging resolutely to their religious traditions. Protestant groups, especially the Baptists with as many as two million members, were attending church services regularly in the major cities.

In his first years of power, Gorbachev concentrated on foreign policy and economic reforms, for the most part ignoring the plight of the churches. Then came a meeting with the Patriarch of Moscow on April 29, 1988. Gorbachev stated his conviction that believers in the Soviet Union should have the full right to express their religious convictions with dignity. He noted that ethics and morals were extremely helpful in the common cause of improving Soviet society. In a TV interview following the meeting with the Patriarch, Gorbachev expressed regrets for "past mistakes made with regard to the Church and believers." On this occasion he announced that a new law to protect religious liberty was being considered.

What brought Gorbachev to this remarkable reversal of long-standing Soviet policy? Born in 1931, he grew up in a religious environment. His mother, a practicing Orthodox Christian throughout her life, had her son baptized. While attending primary and secondary schools in southern Russia, he was exposed to an atheistic line of thought. His law studies at Moscow State University from 1950 to 1955 included a compulsory course on scientific atheism.

Although Gorbachev now describes himself as an atheist, it is possible that he retained some sense of the spiritual power of the Orthodox Christianity which he learned from his mother. There is no doubt that he recognized a spiritual aspect to *perestroika*. He noted this connection in his conversations with Pope John Paul II and repeated it on a number of occasions. In his farewell address, he suggested that one of his most important accomplishments was to have freed his society "politically and spiritually."

How did he do that? In 1990 Gorbachev got the Supreme Soviet to pass legislation giving religious organizations equality under the law and freedom from state interference. Citizens now have constitutional rights to profess any religion or none, to teach religion at home or in private schools, to acquire and use religious literature, to secure the moral upbringing and training of their children, and to conduct their ceremonies in churches, apartments or houses.

Even before the passage of this legislation, Gorbachev's *glasnost* policy had made possible an immense millenial celebration of the coming of Christianity to Kiev. This anniversary commemorated the baptism of Prince Vladimir and his people in 988 and their wholehearted embrace of the Christian faith which his emissaries had brought back from Constantinople. In June of 1988 over 1,500 religious leaders from all over the world, including the Archbishop of Canterbury and Vatican representative Cardinal Willebrands, assembled in Moscow at the restored Danilov Monastery a mile south of the Kremlin. They celebrated with Orthodox Christians the thousand-year history of a religious tradition which produced a rich culture and continues to shape the imaginations of millions of people.

The celebration included a Council of the Orthodox Church. The council canonized a number of saints, including Andrei Rublev, the 15th-century monk who painted the famous icons of the Holy Trinity and the Savior. The council also passed legislation which restored the leadership role of parish priests in the ongoing life of their parishes.

On June 16 the celebration moved to Kiev. There an immense throng of people stood for hours in the rain to commemorate the baptism of St. Vladimir, their apostle and model of charity.

The millennium sparked a remarkable religious revival in the Soviet Union. In the following year, 800 new Orthodox communities were established. Young people who had followed the celebration on national television began searching for answers not provided by their atheistic training. Seminaries were reopened with as many as 2,500 students enrolled. Monasteries were restored. Religious leaders were elected to legislative bodies. (This trend continues as the Patriarch of Moscow and other clerics now serve in the Russian Parliament.) The Ukrainian Catholic Church, illegal since 1946, resurfaced with renewed vigor.

Mikhail Gorbachev played a major role in unleashing this amazing burst of spiritual energy. I like to compare him to Pope John XXIII. Both worked their way up through a rigid system, functioning effectively within its parameters until they reached the top. Due to their breadth of vision, they were able to see the limitations of their respective institutions and, through great political skills, were able to accomplish important reforms. Their progressive programs are linked in the popular mind with key words: Pope John XXIII's with *aggorniamento* and Gorbachev with *glasnost* and *perestroika*. Both had to deal with conservative elements within their bureaucratic structures, periodically giving in to them on relatively minor matters in order to get major changes. These two great leaders have left a legacy of greater openness and also a continuing challenge to make their initial reforms more effective.

Religious groups in the former Soviet Union now have a new set of problems. The Orthodox and the Catholics in the Ukraine are fighting over church buildings. The mainline Churches are afraid of the influx of aggressive Christian evangelicals invading their territory. In some places reluctant local officials are refusing to return church buildings. Christian Armenians and Muslim Azerbaijoni are involved in a bloody conflict over territory. The dwindling Jewish community still suffers from anti-Semitism. Many religious communities find themselves drawn into nationalistic machinations and ethnic disputes.

Despite these problems, a new and vital spirit has been released. The challenge for the Churches is to seize the moment and play a constructive force in continuing the process of liberation made possible by the reforms of Mikhail Gorbachev.

6. Muslim Students: A Step Toward World Peace

During the Persian Gulf war, many Christians in the United States realized once again how little they know about the Islamic religious tradition. It has always been hard for the West to understand the role Islam plays in the cultural and political affairs of Middle Eastern countries.

We paid a heavy price for failing to recognize the influence of Islamic fundamentalism on Iranian policies. The strife in Lebanon is difficult to assess without understanding the relationship between Christians and Muslims in that country. The antipathy between Sunni and Shiite Muslims in Iraq is an important element in sorting out the political situation in the Middle East. The politics of Libya become more intelligible when we consider the disputes between Muammar al-Qaddafi and Muslim religious leaders.

A good case can be made that the quest for world peace now hinges on an improved understanding between the Christian West and the Muslim East. It is therefore important for us to gain a deeper knowledge of Islam so that we can avoid stereotypical thinking and learn to cooperate with Muslims on the basis of genuine understanding.

As Christians open to dialogue, we need a broad understanding of the Islamic tradition. Islam is based on revelations received by the prophet Muhammad from the Angel Gabriel beginning in C.E. 610 in a cave near Mecca, which is in modern-day Saudi Arabia. These revelations were eventually written down and form Islam's holy book, the *Qur'an*, which guides the religious understanding and conduct of all Muslims.

The *Qur'an* teaches that there is only one God, Allah, who has no equals or partners. This God, who spoke through all the true prophets of Judaism and Christianity—such as Abraham, Moses and Jesus—chose Muhammad to be the final prophet, or messenger, to all humankind. All Muslims are bound to accept the divine message in the *Qur'an* and to fight for the cause of Allah by spreading his message to the whole world.

The most important duties of Muslim believers are summed up in the Five Pillars of Islam: (1) faith in the one God, Allah, and Muhammad as his prophet; (2) formal prayer five times a day, including the communal prayer in the mosque at noon on Fridays; (3) fasting during the month of Ramadan; (4) almsgiving to help the poor; and (5) a pilgrimage to Mecca at least once in a lifetime.

In 622 Muhammad, facing severe opposition in his hometown of Mecca, was forced to flee to Medina. This flight, known as the Hijra, is regarded as the beginning of Islam as a religion. By the time Muhammad died in 632, Islam had already spread throughout Iraq and North Africa. This amazing expansion continued throughout the next century, spreading as far as Spain and parts of India.

Islam experienced a schism in the late seventh century which led to the formation of the minority Shiite sect. This Shiite minority continues to exist alongside the Sunni majority. Islam today has an estimated one billion members and is represented in practically every country.

The large number of Muslim students who attend colleges and universities in the United States provide an excellent resource for those interested in getting to know more about how the teachings of Islam are actually appropriated by ordinary people. My strongest impression from the Muslim students I have known over the years is that they have a tremendous passion and enthusiasm for their religious heritage.

I recall participating in a Christian-Muslim dialogue initiated by Muslim students interested in generating a greater understanding and appreciation of each religion. The format was simple: A visiting lecturer would give a presentation on the role of the *Qur'an* in Islam, and I would talk about the function of the Bible in the Catholic tradition. The presentations were to be followed by questions and general discussion.

Almost 300 students showed up and about 90 percent were Muslims. The audience was extremely attentive during the presentations and the responses to the numerous written questions submitted. When the floor was opened for oral comments, many of the Muslim students took advantage of the opportunity to attack some of the points I had made about Christianity.

After the moderator terminated the formal discussion, which had already lasted over three hours, I was surrounded by enthusiastic Muslim students who wanted to carry on the conversation. They offered a fascinating mix of politically-slanted comments, vigorous repudiations of my presentation, popular explanations of their own beliefs and personal witnessing. This informal discussion remained civil and quite cordial. They were genuinely appreciative of my participation in the dialogue, and it seemed that we had established some rapport in this short space of time. Even as I disengaged myself from the group to head for home, some of the students continued to follow me and carry on the discussion.

Seldom, if ever, have I experienced such passionate concern about religious matters. For Muslims, religion is not just one area of life to be discussed objectively. Religion is at the heart of their whole personal and cultural self-understanding. It is a matter of ultimate concern.

A second impression gleaned from my encounters with Muslim students is that they have appropriated Islam in a very deep but uncritical way. They have not passed through anything like the European Enlightenment which moved Western Christians to challenge Church authority, to insist on personal decisions in religious matters and to recognize theological pluralism. Discussions with Muslim students remind me of similar conversations with pre-Vatican II Catholics who believed that the Church was monolithic, that the Scriptures were free of error, that doctrines were to be taken literally and that the pope could do no wrong.

A prime example of this uncritical Muslim approach occurred during the question period after another dialogue session. I had made the point that Christians speak of Jesus Christ not only as an ethical teacher but as the son of God. One young woman, seated in the back of the hall with all the Muslim women, posed this question: "If Jesus was the son of God, then who was God's wife?"

I chose to interpret the question as an honest inquiry, using the opportunity to explain that all religious language is symbolic and points to the mystery that is beyond all words, categories and images. Our language about God cannot be taken literally but must be understood as pointing to something true, if ultimately mysterious, about the deity. When we call God our Father, we do not mean that he is male or has produced children or has a wife. I suggested to the students that when they call Allah the Supreme Judge, they are not suggesting that he operates in a courtroom.

My explanation of the function of religious language drew strong negative responses from the Muslim students. They insisted that Islam was rigorously logical and reasonable. They did not have to resort to the language of mystery and symbol to defend their religion, as I did with Christianity. They emphasized Islam's clear ethical commands and showed no interest in the Suffi mystical tradition spawned by Islam. Their concern was to present a strong defense of the truth claims of Islam based on rational argumentation.

The students likewise insisted that the *Qur'an* is the absolutely inerrant word of God and should be interpreted literally. They showed no knowledge of variant readings of the original text or of the work of contemporary Muslim scholars on historical-critical approaches to the Scriptures. In this regard they sound very much like contemporary Christian fundamentalists.

The Muslims in the dialogue not only rejected my emphasis on mystery, symbolic language and biblical criticism, but they were genuinely puzzled by the Church-State distinction operative in the United States. For them religion and culture are indivisible, and a theocratic form of government is the logical consequence. They insisted, however, that in a Muslim theocracy Christianity, and other religions as well, have freedom to worship in their own way.

Religion exists not in the minds of scholars but in the lived experience of believers. We come to know the deeper meaning of Islam by observing how Muslims live and by listening to the way they explain their faith.

Some cautions are in order, however, in dialogue with Muslim students. As a minority in a Christian country, they have a tendency to present a united front and play down any differences within Islam. They are also understandably cautious about admitting any failures or mistakes within their religious tradition.

There is a greater pluralism within Islam, however, than dialogue with international students might indicate. Enlightened Muslim scholars, for example, speak more openly about divisions within Islam, about political disputes, about various interpretations of passages in the *Qur'an* and about failures to live up to Islamic ideals.

Despite these cautions, I have found my encounters with Muslim students to be stimulating and enlightening. They are passionate about religion and totally dedicated to their faith. Islam, for them, is a total worldview, a comprehensive system for interpreting and integrating their experiences. They find genuine enlightenment and inspiration in the *Qur'an*.

From our Christian perspective, we can interpret and appreciate this Muslim faith as the fruit of God's saving grace. Islam is indeed a powerful religious tradition which reminds all of us of the need for total surrender to the one God who is compassionate and merciful. Muhammad was indeed a great prophet who spoke out courageously against injustice and called on all to do the will of God. The Islamic tradition is often known in the West for its aggressive tendencies. But at Islam's core are deep religious sensibilities and a compassionate spirit which have produced magnificent cultures.

We Christians should enter into dialogue with Muslims, convinced that we can learn important truths about the divine-human relationship from each other. Given the tensions in the world today, mutual understanding and cooperation among the great religious traditions is no longer an interfaith luxury. It has become a practical necessity in the search for a just and enduring peace.

7. Muhammad and Jesus:
A Positive Assessment

As part of the effort to overcome lingering ignorance and prejudice between Christians and Muslims, I recently participated in a series of discussions with Muslim scholars and students at the University of Toledo. My task was to address the question of similarities and differences from the Christian viewpoint. In preparation, I turned to a book entitled *Christianity and the World Religions: Paths to Dialogue with Islam, Hinduism and Buddhism,* written by Hans Küng in conjunction with scholars representing various religious traditions.

In my presentation, I stressed the common bond we Christians have with Muslims and Jews as monotheists who believe in the *one God,* variously called Yahweh, Abba and Allah. For all of us in the monotheistic family, faith involves a whole-hearted surrender to God and God's Word. Faith involves a reasonable trust in the one God who gives life and meaning to all things. Thus Christians unite with Muslims in opposing all human attempts to create idols by turning preliminary concerns into ultimate ones.

Talk of Trinity smacks of tritheism to Muslims. It is common for them to argue that the Trinity is not found in the Bible but is only a later doctrinal development. These Islamic challenges remind us to present trinitarian doctrine in a way which preserves our fundamental biblical notion that there is one God, Creator and Judge of all. We can, for example, speak of the one and only God as the Father who is the source of all things, the Word who is personally present in history, and as the Spirit who is our inner illumination and guide.

With our Muslim and Jewish friends, we Christians also believe in the *God of history*. This God is totally in charge of the world and yet is nearer to us than our own carotid artery, as the *Qur'an* puts it. This God is a gracious and merciful partner to whom we can speak in prayer, offering praise and gratitude. Before this great God we remain free, responsible for our actions and accountable at the judgment.

Christian scholars have affirmed many positive things about Muhammad (570-632). I tried to summarize these in my presentation. Christians can, for example, recognize Muhammad's religious achievement in bringing monotheism to the Arab people, as well as his political accomplishments in unifying the Arab peninsula. Clearly he raised the ethical standards of his times and overcame many of the social abuses.

Within the framework of contemporary theology, it is possible to think of Muhammad as a genuine prophet who correctly interpreted important aspects of the divine-human relationship. He was a man committed to God and faithful to his task as Allah's messenger. His sense of submission to the merciful Judge enabled him to stand up against the ruling class and to work diligently on behalf of his people.

Muhammad delivered a message with tremendous universal appeal. Today it binds an estimated one billion people together in the simple faith that there is no God but Allah and Muhammad is his prophet. Its five fundamental duties include professing the faith, regular prayer, almsgiving, a month of fasting and a pilgrimage to Mecca. Christians assessing this great religious tradition can affirm it as a continuing source of inspiration and guidance for its followers and as a genuine vehicle of truth and salvation.

We also recognize Muhammad as the inspiration behind the *Qur'an*, a sacred book that is both inspired and inspiring. It totally informs Islamic life and provides Muslims with a fundamental law. This book can be seen as an authentic source of God's revelation.

Finally, we Christians can recognize Muhammad as an impressive human being. He exemplies for Muslims the life of virtue to which they aspire.

Muslims, of course, go beyond this positive Christian assessment. They insist that Muhammad is the definitive messenger of God who delivered a universal message which is to be accepted by all people.

Some Muslims claim that the Bible contains prophecies about the coming of Muhammad. They see Muhammad as the last messenger, descended from Abraham through Ishmael, who also received from God a promise to become a great nation (Genesis 21:13, 18). They see fulfilled in Muhammad Yahweh's promise to Moses to "raise up a prophet like yourself for them from their own brothers" (Deuteronomy 18:18). Moreover, Muslims who probe the Bible in this fashion often identify Muhammad as the Paraclete, or Comforter, that Jesus promised would be sent by the Father to teach new things (John 16:4-15).

When this biblical line of argument was advanced in our discussion, I argued that it was an improper use of the Bible. The biblical authors had a message for the people of their times which has a universal significance and offers a general hope for the future. They did not make specific predictions of future events—whether the coming of the prophet Muhammad six centuries after Jesus, as Muslims claim, or the date of the end of the world, as some fundamentalist Christians claim.

In dialogue with Muslims, it is important for Christians to recognize the positive assessment of Jesus found in the *Qur'an*. He comes into the world through a virgin birth, preaches the truth, works miracles with God's permission and lives an exemplary life of prayer and almsgiving. His message was rejected, and the Jews tried to crucify him but failed. Finally, God raised him up to heaven.

In my presentation I tried to express appreciation for this positive picture of Jesus, while at the same time stressing that the Gospels give us a much fuller picture. Jesus taught a radical ethic of love which calls us to forgive even our enemies. He opposed every kind of legalism, insisting on a religion of the heart. His teachings incurred the wrath of the authorities and led to his death on the cross—an historical fact attested to by all the New Testament writers and by the Roman historian Tacitus.

For Christians, Jesus is not the precursor for Muhammad but the definitive prophet, the bringer of the kingdom. Just as the *Qur'an* is the Word of God for Muslims, so for Christians Jesus is God's Word manifest in human form. Jesus reveals to us a God who is not only creator and judge, but who also loves us intimately and has compassion for all human beings. While Muhammad lived a successful life as a prophet and statesman, Jesus met with failure and was crucified because he was faithful to the call of his Father. In Jesus, we come to know the God who transforms death into eternal life and provides meaning in the midst of all the absurdities which assail us.

Despite these differences the two religious traditions can learn from one another. Islam reminds Christians that we dare not create idols to rival the one God and that our faith and everyday life must form an integrated whole. Muslims who reflect on the biblical understanding of Jesus might be helped to keep Islamic law in proper perspective and to put greater emphasis on the loving compassion exercised by the great God.

In my concluding remarks, I asked the Muslims present whether they were ready to take a more critical look at their tradition, including the treatment of women in Islamic countries. Their general response was represented by one young woman attired in traditional Muslim dress who appeared to me to be a Western convert to Islam. She described her marriage to a Muslim husband as entirely satisfying and devoid of any hints of inequality. She insisted that Muslim women have equal rights and opportunities and are not in any way second-class citizens—a positive assessment which seemed to meet with total agreement among the Muslims present.

In the continuing dialogue after the formal discussion ended, I could find no aspect of Islam, no teaching of the *Qur'an*, no religiously-based practices which provoked the slightest hint of disagreement or criticism. When I spoke about bias against women in the Catholic community, about a lingering history of anti-Semitism, about the excesses of the Crusades, they responding by extolling the virtues of Islam and by insisting that this proved that Muhammad was truly God's final messenger.

I loved the passion of these students and the stimulation of the whole discussion. I commended them for achieving an admirable integration of faith and life. But I also recognized how much we Western Christians are a product of the Enlightenment and the beneficiaries of a long tradition of criticism and dialogue which searches for a truth greater than anyone currently possesses.

If we want world peace, we must promote interfaith dialogue and cooperation. Dialogue between the Christian and Muslim community will not be easy, but it will be well worth the effort.

8. Buddhists: Practical Wisdom for Westerners

I had come by Shinkeinnon bullet train from Tokyo to Kyoto to give a series of lectures to Maryknoll missionaries from all over Japan. A Maryknoll priest with a great deal of experience in Christian-Buddhist dialogue had arranged a meeting for me with a Buddhist monk who lived in the world-famous Enryaku-ji monastery established at the top of Mt. Hiei in the late eighth century. The cable car ride up the mountain on this beautiful late August day provided a marvelous view of the beautiful city of Kyoto, a major cultural center spared massive Allied bombing during World War II, and of Lake Biwa, the largest lake in Japan.

I hoped this dialogue would take me to the heart of the Buddhist tradition. I had already gotten some feel for the popular religion by visiting a number of Buddhist temples and asking people why they performed certain rituals, such as purifying themselves with water or burning incense. A fascinating discussion with Buddhist students at Sophia University in Tokyo had brought me into contact with a more sophisticated and less magical version of the tradition. Reading books such as *The Emptying God: A Buddhist-Jewish-Christian Conversation*, edited by John Cobb and Christopher Ives (Orbis, 1990), had given me a glimpse of the world of Buddhist scholarship. But I realized that the monks living in monasteries have appropriated the teachings and the spirit of Buddhism in a way that nonpracticing scholars and most lay persons cannot.

Siddhartha Gautama (c. 563-486 B.C.E.), who became known as the Buddha, taught a practical wisdom while refusing to speculate about ultimately mysterious questions. His four noble truths stressed the fact of suffering, located its cause in human craving, and suggested concrete means to overcome these desires. These practical methods, which include renunciation of the world, ascetical practices and extensive meditation leading to enlightenment (*satori*), can best be followed in the context of monastic living. It is through monasticism that authentic Buddhism is preserved and taught. Buddhist monks know things that escape both scholars and ordinary believers.

The Reverend Sasaki impressed me from the first moment he entered the tastefully-decorated room. He was a strong, vigorous, animated man with an obvious confidence and inner serenity. After the formal introductions by our skillful Maryknoll translator, he told me about Dengyo Daishi, the founder of the monastery. His systematic training regimen for his followers is still in use today.

Daishi's spirit and message are reflected in his famous saying: "Till the bright age of the coming Buddha, keep the light of the *dharma* [fundamental teaching] shining." To symbolize this teaching, the monks have kept three ceremonial lamps burning for the past 1,200 years. Known as "The Inextinguishable Dharma Lights," they remain before the main altar in the magnificent Central Hall.

Since its founding in the eighth century, this monastery has kept alive this ideal of forming enlightened persons who illumine their surroundings. Throughout the centuries the monastery has functioned as the sacred center of Japanese Mahayana Buddhism and as a major influence on Zen Buddhism. Many eminent Buddhist scholars have studied there and thousands of visitors continue to come to the monastery each year. In August of 1987, religious leaders from all over the world assembled at the monastery for a conference on world peace.

With this background in mind, I asked the Reverend Sasaki about his meditation practices. He pointed out the great importance of disciplined training. Along with the other full-fledged monks, he had undergone the 12-year training period prescribed by Dengyo Daishi. This includes a 92-day exercise in meditation during which the novice constantly maintains the lotus position without lying down to sleep or getting up to eat. A current monk known for his piety has repeated this intensive period on 10 different occasions.

While emphasizing the importance of physical posture in meditation, Sasaki got down on the floor and demonstrated the proper way to assume the lotus position. He spoke at great length about the importance of concentrating on breathing during meditation—a method calculated to empty one's mind. He did not use a mantra in connection with his breathing—and seemed to dismiss the value of such a repetitive practice. He spoke personally about his approach to distractions, especially his efforts to be gentle with himself after learning the hard way that rigidity is counterproductive. Just go back and concentrate on your breathing, he advised.

In good Buddhist fashion, he insisted that the only way to really learn about meditation is to actually do it regularly and systematically. Proper training is crucial. Short cuts are impossible.

Sasaki also insisted on the great importance of discipline and asceticism. He described for me the so-called "thousand-day mountain pilgrimage." A monk walks by himself 4,000 kilometers through the mountains surrounding Kyoto for 1,000 days over a period of seven years. The exact purpose of this ordeal was not clear to me, but it reminded me of the wilderness experiences designed to help individuals learn how to survive difficult circumstances on their own.

The daily routine at the monastery also provides a framework for a disciplined way of life. The monks arise at 5 a.m. and meditate for an hour as a group. Throughout the day they engage in intense study and private meditation. These disciplines are not an end in themselves, but are part of the whole process of achieving enlightenment. The daily regimen is designed to help the monks uncover illusions and be attentive to what is at hand at the moment. The long, rigorous reflection on a personal koan, or radically enigmatic puzzle (for example, "What is it that carries me all day?") challenges their ordinary perceptions of reality and prepares them for enlightenment.

All these ascetic practices, along with the long hours of meditation, enable the monks to get rid of their ego and achieve the radical insight that even the self is illusory. For Buddhists there is no permanent fixed essence called a "self" but only the flux and flow of process. During the course of this explanation it became clear to me that enlightenment is itself a process and that Sasaki was still probing the meaning of his own breakthrough in consciousness.

When I brought up the question of God, his whole demeanor changed. His face went blank. It was as though he did not understand the question. I posed the question in many ways, asking about the nature of the ultimate, the deepest purpose of meditation, the source of his moral convictions and the ultimate goals of the enlightenment process. I am not sure if he really did not understand my questions or if his reactions were his practiced way of informing me that the questions were irrelevant. At any rate, his responses reflected the Buddhist conviction that it is better to be silent about the great metaphysical questions.

When I turned to the more practical matter of world peace, he became animated once again. He had been very involved in the 1987 religious summit conference at the monastery, and he was extremely proud of his Buddhist community in initiating and organizing the conference. He showed me a picture of the important dignitaries who had attended from all over the world, including cardinals from the Vatican. He believes that world peace depends on personal peace. If individuals can get rid of ego and become more serene, they will practice compassion and radiate peace to the larger community.

Finally, I brought up the scholarly dialogue between Christians and Buddhists centered in the so-called Kyoto school which has, for many decades, tried to explain Buddhism in terms congenial to the Western philosophical mind. The Buddhist scholar Masao Abe had recently prompted an important discussion by relating the Buddhist concept of "Emptiness" to Paul's teaching in Philippians which speaks of Jesus emptying himself and taking on the form of a slave. Sasaki was really not interested in this dialogue. He seemed to feel that the Kyoto school, which I find so helpful, is unfaithful to Buddhist principles because they have become too Westernized.

This stimulating dialogue with the Reverend Sasaki ended all too soon, but it gave me a touchstone for interpreting my other encounters with Buddhism throughout Japan. I recalled the inherent power of the Buddhist tradition when I visited the gigantic statue of the Buddha in the city of Nara where it is enshrined in the largest wooden structure in the world. The total dedication of the monks gave me a standard for measuring the divided allegiances of Buddhist students at Sophia University who told me they were born Shinto, intended to have Western-style Christian weddings, but would eventually die as Buddhists. The purity of the monastic ideal brought into focus the magical notion of religion I encountered at the Sensoji Buddhist temple in Tokyo where individuals used incense to ward off evil powers and prayed to the popular god Kannon to save them from harm. And most significantly, while meditating at the graceful Temple of the Golden Pavilion in Kyoto, I experienced a moment of serenity which seemed to link me with the spirit of Buddhist monasticism.